Susie & Otto C

BIG
FAT
LOVE

The Book of Possibilities

Published by Conscious Heart Publishing
P.O. Box 14544
Columbus, Ohio 43214
614-568-8282

Paperback ISBN: 978-0-9725130-05
Digital ISBN: 978-09725130-1-2

"When I die, God is not going to say, 'You stole a candy bar when you were five.' He is going to say, 'You learned to love. I like that.'"

Steve Hardison

The Invitation

The Choice for Love in Every Moment

You have a choice in every moment. That choice determines everything about every relationship, every interaction you have with another person, how much (or how little) you connect with other people and how much love you have in your life.

And this choice is something that is so simple and so profound that you might never see it and its potential for awakening more love and possibilities in your relationships and life.

The choice is simply this:

Will you open as love in this moment and allow new possibilities to appear in fresh, new ways for you?

Or

Will you close your heart, mind and soul and allow the fears, doubts, insecurities and negative stories you believe to run the show and cut off the flow of love, possibilities and miracles in your life?

The thoughts that you, and any of us, believe can take you away from love and possibilities.

It happens so quickly, so innocently and with such certainty that you don't realize that you're simply caught up in believing a thought in the moment that has temporarily hijacked your thinking.

That thinking we're talking about is the same thinking that led you to shut down and wall yourself off in big and small ways. That thinking led you to believe that this is your best move to help you get what you want from love and life.

And that couldn't be more wrong.

Opening instead of closing, finding kindness instead of anger, discovering love instead of fear, and creating passion instead of boredom always comes down to what you are seeing and making real in this (and every) moment.

What if you realized that all that's ever going on for you and every single one of us is that you're living in each moment from the experience of the thoughts you believe and make real?

And it's a choice.

This book is our loving invitation to help you open to more love than you ever thought possible and to continue to nourish it.

Our invitation to you about love is THIS:

Don't wait.

Don't wait for that other person to open their heart first.

You go first.

If they won't or can't open their heart just yet, you open your heart first.

You can never know what pain that other person is going through, what story they're holding onto that's causing them to act like they are or why they can't find the courage to open first.

You can decide that opening your heart and keeping it open is more important than keeping it closed and shutting out love.

This isn't a contest of wills to see who can outlast the other shut down love the longest.

You never want to shut down your heart and put up a force field just to prove a point, make them pay or show them how wrong they are.

The two of us have played that game and nobody wins.

The goal in every relationship you find yourself in is to connect your hearts, love deeper and continue to do that over and over again until God or the Great Spirit says, "Times up."

Decide that love is worth it and always choose love over fear, doubt and separation.

Don't wait.

Consciously decide to hold nothing back.

Bring all of you.

Start now by reading this book and read it about you.

You can read it from cover to cover or skip around and randomly choosing the ideas and topics that resonate with you.

However you choose, our suggestion is to read it with an open heart and open mind.

This was a collaboration of love with some chapters written solely by Otto, some by Susie and others together to give you, the reader, a deeper experience of how to expand your vision of what's possible.

You'll also notice that we've not included a question or suggestion to focus on at the end of each chapter. This is on purpose so that you're free to focus on whatever holds the greatest possibility for you inside that particular chapter.

This book is for YOU.

What we can tell you about love and possibilities is this:

All you need is a small crack in the doorway of your heart to be able to let the light of love enter your life in deeper and more profound ways.

All you need to experience true "love miracles" and have them show up in your life on a regular basis is a willingness to allow them in your daily life, as well as a willingness to both look for them as you go about your day and the eyes to notice them when they do show up.

That's our sincere wish for you!

Blessings and Love to you,

Susie and Otto Collins

Table of Contents

Chapter 1
The Wake Up Call
By Otto

My great desire for you and your life is that you find something, like I did, that wakes you up to more possibilities for love in your life.

Sometimes wake up calls to possibilities can be soft and subtle and sometimes they can be thunderous, loud and unmistakable.

My wake up call to more, higher and deeper possibilities for love came in 1996 when I was 14 years into a marriage that was running out of steam.

There was nothing wrong with the person I was married to.

I thought conflict, distance, pain, martyrdom, lack of closeness, lack of connection and lack of intimacy were all normal.

I thought it was normal for passion in a marriage to die or fade away over the years.

I saw my future and thought, "There's gotta be more possible with love than this. I gotta find a way to create something better."

I wanted something more, something different from what we knew how to create.

I spent many late nights thinking, hoping, wishing, praying and asking for how I could have the love in my life that I so desperately wanted but didn't have.

My answer came in the form of two books.

The first was a book by Kenny and Julia Loggins called *The Unimaginable Life* and the second was *Seat of The Soul* by Gary Zukav.

After I read these two books, my sense of possibilities for a new, different, expanded version of love was never the same.

In *The Unimaginable Life*, I learned that two people could actually talk about ANYTHING and still feel close and connected without shutting down for days or weeks at a time.

I was seeing that passion, love and intimacy could be exciting, thrilling and that you could still be filled with desire for another person even after being together for years.

This could even be true when there are big differences between the two of you and chaos is swirling around you.

In *Seat of The Soul*, I learned about "Spiritual Partnerships" and how it was possible for two people to come together as equals in a relationship created intentionally, by design and for the purpose of growing together personally and spiritually.

With what I was learning, my heart, my mind and my soul were so stretched, so blown wide open with new possibilities that I knew I could no longer settle for a love that didn't make me come alive any more.

I saw that the doors of possibility could swing open so much wider than I had seen up until that point.

Even though I didn't know how at the time, I knew, whether it was with the person I was with (or with someone else), I was going to have BIG love in my life.

This new internal desire to have big love became a commitment so strong that I was willing to literally do anything to have it.

For me, it turned out to be with the woman I call the "Incredible Susie."

As of this writing, this is year 25 for us and our love and our life together just keep getting better and better.

For you, it could be with the person you're already in a relationship with or it could be with someone you haven't met yet.

What I do know is THIS:

More love is available to you than you can see right now.

THIS is your wake up call.

Chapter 2
Learning to Love More Deeply By Susie

Like Otto, I didn't know what was possible about how expansive love could be in my life until I allowed myself to see beyond my past.

I was married to my first husband for 30 years. Not a bad marriage, but it was held together by the comfort of our shared history, which included our daughter, rather than the spiritual partner and connection I craved.

A few weeks after my soon-to-be ex left our home, I had a pivotal moment while standing alone in my living room. I looked past the grief of the end of my marriage and allowed myself to see the possibility of a love for me that I'd only glimpsed in other couples.

Like the time I saw a couple sitting several rows in front of me at a play.

Oblivious to whether anyone else was watching, they were laughing with their heads intimately close together and I said to myself,

"I want that!"

It wasn't until after our divorce that I could allow myself to open to creating a different kind of intimate relationship for my future, one that fed my spiritual growth and my soul.

To my surprise, shortly after my first marriage ended, Otto and I started on our amazing journey of learning to love one another in wondrous ways that keep unfolding.

In the process of truly opening my heart, learning to communicate better and loving Otto more deeply and with more compassion, a funny thing happened.

I started loving myself and others in a deeper way as well.

Over the years, I've found myself slowing down, not jumping to untrue conclusions as quickly and not getting as defensive as I once did.

I've been discovering a deeper well of curiosity inside me and a desire to connect with whomever I come into contact with, including Otto.

I've also been allowing love for myself to grow and it's showing up in who I'm being with others more and more of the time.

The exciting thing about all of this is that I know that new possibilities for love aren't just available to me.

They're available to you and to everyone if you allow them to appear.

"You Are Always
Worthy of Love.
Always. No Exceptions."

Otto Collins

Chapter 3
Love Worthy By Otto

If I'm being completely honest, sometimes I think God, the universe (or whatever name you use for our Creator) hates me.

Sometimes I throw these big temper tantrums inside myself when things don't seem to be going my way or I don't know what to do next to "make" my life go the way I want it to be.

In those moments, I think something must be wrong with me or I came from the factory with a defect or even worse. I'm the child of God who's not loved as much as the others.

I don't get outwardly angry but I do get upset, brooding and quiet in those moments.

And then I remember what I read in the book, *The Way of Mastery* published by the Shanti Christo Foundation, that is true and true always.

And it's THIS:

"I am loved, I am loving and I am lovable forever."

Think about those words for a moment and really take them in.

Remembering this truth always snaps me back to another truth about love and relationships.

Everyone is worthy of love

Even when you forget

Even when you don't see it

Even when you're full of doubt, judgment and self-criticism

Even when you wish love was showing up differently for you than it is right now.

It's easy to forget that you're human and you have bad moments, bad days or maybe even that you've had a bad decade or two.

And yet,

When it comes to the question, "AM I worthy of love?"

There's no one in the sky above looking down on us and deciding who is worthy of love and who's not.

You're the only one who gets to decide that.

You.

Just you.

No one else.

That's it.

We're all worthy of as much love as we can stand in our lives and as much love as we decide we are willing to let in.

Whether or not you are love worthy is simply your choice in every moment.

This is really good news because just as much love is available to you and you are just as "love worthy" as anyone else on the planet.

You get to decide the answer to the question of whether you're worthy of love or not.

And the true answer is of course you are.

You just have to see that.

The truth about love is this:

Love is a gift we are all given.

Love is always there.

You don't have to DO anything to get love.

You ARE love.

Love is always flowing in you, around you and through you unless you are blocking the flow of it.

Love always looks the same.

Love always looks different.

Love never ends.

There's an endless supply of it.

Love isn't dependent on someone or something else.

Love is the essence of who we are.

Love doesn't play favorites.

Love Just Is.

You are THAT.

Chapter 4
Big Fat Love

"Big Fat Love" is a term we made up to describe what's possible for love in your life.

Here's how it got created and what's possible for you.

When the two of us were new in our relationship, Otto gave Susie a card to honor one of the "anniversaries" we celebrate each year.

In fact, we loved the card so much that we remember it and talk about it to this day which is almost 25 years later.

On the front of the card is a graphic of a big, overgrown heart and the words,

"Their Love Was Big and Fat"

And when you open up the card to the middle, there's a cartoon picture of a happy couple and the words,

"Because they fed it a lot between meals."

Think about that for a moment because those two sentences can be the difference between whether your love grows, evolves, and expands or it becomes like the average relationship after the "honeymoon period" is over and becomes "normal" and just plain stale.

The key here is the second part of this sentence where the happy couple "fed their relationship between meals."

In other words, if you want to expand the possibilities for your love, feed it a lot. Not only when you celebrate special occasions, but always.

The same thing applies in all other kinds of relationships.

If you want a closer friendship or connection with someone—a partner, family member or friend—feed that relationship.

What does feeding the love between meals mean?

For a relationship you want to grow or expand

- It means spending time with that person.
- It means deeply listening to him or her.
- It means finding ways to connect, even when you are separated by time, distance or work schedules.
- It means going beyond your comfort zone to do things together or explore new interests.
- It means constantly building that other person up instead of putting them down.
- It means looking for the good, not only in that other person but also in you.
- It means recognizing what you like, love and appreciate about them and letting them know how important they are to you.
- It means choosing to find ways to build passion, intimacy and connection with a partner.
- It means being kinder to yourself, as well as to the other person, and not getting defensive.

- It means being willing to see that other person's point of view without feeling like you have to correct them, make them wrong or change them in some way.
- It can mean anything that will fill the relationship with more love, including loving yourself more of the time.

But what If you want a new love to come into your life that isn't here yet?

Feed your possibilities instead of your impossibilities.

To expand your possibilities for a love you want but don't yet have, start by loving yourself and letting go of anything within you that's keeping love away.

Otto once had a coaching client who associated so much emotional pain to the idea of opening herself up to new love that she would get physically sick every time she thought about accepting someone's invitation to go on a date or even meet up at a local coffee shop.

Although this woman had a lot going for her in her life, she simply wasn't open to seeing any new possibilities around new love.

Whatever your circumstances, this doesn't have to be you if you want more love in your life.

Our experience tells us that if you look for anything in life, you'll be certain to find it, including Big Fat Love.

You can start creating miracles in your love life and in all of your relationships.

Beginning right now, if that is what you want.

Just make sure you feed your love and your possibilities more and more of the time.

Chapter 5
What Matters Most

There is a famous quote we just love from Stephen Covey the author of the book *7 Habits of Highly Effective People* that says,

"What matters most should never be at the mercy of what matters least."

Let's quickly take a look at what matters most in creating more possibilities in love.

It's simple really.

In any moment, what matters most is always what will bring you and that other person closer together instead of moving you further apart.

That's it.

Just like you in any relationship you're in, we always want to be doing things that help us create a BIG FAT LOVE. Sometimes it can be so easy to innocently do something that takes you away from that.

Possibilities skyrocket when the other person feels seen, heard and cared for instead of unappreciated, not desired and disconnected from you.

Possibilities become greater when you look for the things you like, love or appreciate about the other person instead of focusing on the parts of them you want to change or make different.

What matters most is the love, the connection and the sincere desire to create something special with each other every single day with each other.

Anything you can do, say or be that furthers this is what matters most. You're going to want to do more of that.

Anything you do or say that takes you away from creating more love is what matters least and is always to be avoided.

For example:

Is it more important to point out who should get the credit for something or to focus on and encourage the two of you to work together?

Is it more important to tell the other person they should lose a few pounds or focus on other aspects of them that are amazing?

Is it more important to bury your truth to keep the peace or see your "truth" and live from that place?

Is it more important to make eye contact and listen when someone you love is speaking or is it more important to get whatever you're involved in done, ignoring him or her?

And finally, would it be more important to be angry, harsh and critical when things go wrong or would it be better to see the other person as a friend, a partner or someone important to you that you care about?

Make a list in your head or on paper of what you start to notice that creates more intimacy, love and connection and do more of that.

And then, keep doing it.

Continue to return to the very simple question,

"What matters most here?"

Just asking this question again and again, especially when you're feeling irritated or feeling any other unsettling emotion, can be a true game-changer for your love and all your relationships.

This can certainly mean expressing yourself in a way that invites the other person to listen and not become defensive.

There's a whole other level that can take you beyond just "doing" things to try to make shifts, changes and improvements in your relationships and love life.

This is the level of whom you are being and that precedes all doing.

In other words, what you do always comes as a result of who you are being and how you are showing up in each moment.

THIS level, the level of BEING, is where real transformation in love, life and relationships is created.

This is what we're talking about in the next chapter: "It's All about Being."

"BEING is everything and ALL doing comes from who you are being."

Steve Hardison

Chapter 6
It's All about Being

What's the first question you ask yourself when faced with a challenging love or relationship situation?

It almost always starts with a "How do I _____?" question.

Like one of these:

"How do I get her to change?"

"How do I get him to open up to me more?"

"How do I attract a partner I really want to be with?"

"How do I find available men?"

"How do I get him to include me when he's making important decisions?"

"How do I communicate my wants and needs to her in a way she understands?"

"How do I get him to want to be more intimate with me?"

"How do I stop being jealous when there's no reason to be?"

We could come up with a hundred questions like these and, while these are all really important, there are much better ones you might want to consider asking yourself instead.

These better questions will ultimately lead you to all the love, connection, intimacy and closeness you could ever want.

They focus you on who you are BEING.

Steve Hardison, the Ultimate Coach, says, "BEING is everything and ALL doing comes from who you are being."

Yes, "doing" does come from who you are "being" and not the other way around.

Here are a few questions we suggest you slowly ask yourself (or just pick one to focus on) that will point you in a Big Fat Love direction:

- "Who would I need to be to create the love in my life that I really want?"
- "Who would I need to be to be a more loving person?"
- "Who would I need to be to love myself more of the time?"
- "Who would I need to be to invite the people in my life to loving conversations instead of having arguments?"
- "Who would I need to be to see the good in others instead of the negative aspects of them?"
- "Who would I need to be to be at peace inside me more of the time?"
- "Who would I need to be to let go of any fears I have that are getting in the way of love expanding in my life?"
- "Who would I have to be to make sure the love I have for the people in my life grows exponentially?"

When one of our coaching clients sat with the question, "Who would I need to be to take my relationship with my boyfriend to the next level?" —

She found that she had to be honest with herself about her greatest desire which was for financial security for herself and her kids that she previously thought would come from moving in together with her boyfriend.

Because of her realization about who she needed to be to have this financial security, she focused instead on expanding her business and relaxed about her future with her boyfriend who'd been less committed than she'd liked.

When you sit with even one of these "being" questions, you open up to possibilities that can change your life.

When you start taking a look at who you are being, the answers always come out of that place deep inside.

When you start focusing more and more on who you are being, the answers to the "doing" questions tend to take care of themselves.

When you focus more and more on who you are being, you'll know what to say and how to "be" in just the right way and in the right timing for expansion of love and connection.

We invite you to sit with the "being" question that applies most to what you want more of in your life or come up with some good ones on your own and watch for the wisdom, the insights and the ideas that come to you.

Love waits on your welcome.

Chapter 7
A New Definition of Soul Mates

We'd never felt anything like it.

As we hugged at the end of our first "date" one evening in December 1997, we had what we now call our "soul mate experience."

Saying our goodbyes for the night, what started out as a simple hug turned into an intense wave of loving energy, hitting both of us and lasting for several hours.

With this feeling we'd never felt before, we knew we were "home" and didn't want it to end.

This energy we're talking about wasn't erotic or sexual but it was a feeling of love and connection that neither of us had ever experienced up until then.

And this "feeling" we experienced that night has never gone away.

In some ways, it's only grown stronger over the years.

This soul mate experience didn't make sense because Susie is 16 years older than Otto and we are really different people in many, many ways.

But this was beyond what made "sense."

We knew we were soul mates who had finally found one another and have been together ever since that night.

But there's much more to the story.

You know what the popular version of a soul mate is, right?

It's that one person out of the 6 billion or so possibilities that you are destined to find and be with, sharing forever a life of perfect romance, bliss and without any problems.

In our experience, this is a totally beautiful story that for most people (including us) has very little truth to it.

So, what if there's another possibility around this whole soul mate idea?

- What if we're all destined to have soul mates who enter our lives for a reason, a season and in some cases, a lifetime?

- What if the intention of a soul mate relationship was never perfection?

- What if a soul mate relationship is an opportunity to learn about being a good partner, being a good person or about how to be in relationship with another human that you couldn't learn any other way?

- What if it is completely normal and natural for there to be problems and challenges to be worked through or figured out in your soul mate relationship?

- What if your soul mate relationship is bliss some of the time and filled with learning and growth opportunities the rest of the time?

- What if, as many researchers claim, there can be more than one soul mate for each of us?

The truth is that a soul mate can look much different from what you think.

The late, great self-help author and motivational speaker Dr. Wayne Dyer once raised the possibility that a soul mate could be someone you can't stand.

Dr. Dyer said there is a possibility that that other person could be someone who is only in your life to help your soul grow and move past certain ways of being or seeing the world.

He went on to suggest that a soul mate could be someone with whom you fight, argue or have challenges on a regular basis but that person was sent into your life to help you learn certain life lessons you wouldn't have been able to learn otherwise.

That definition certainly broadens and humanizes the old, romanticized idea of a soul mate, doesn't it?

Here's what we've discovered in our years together as soul mates:

Relationships aren't an accident whether you're with someone you consider to be a soul mate or not!

They are a creation.

Soul mates or not, we're sure that if the two of us hadn't committed to learning how to communicate better, be less reactive and grow together as spiritual partners, our marriage would have ended in divorce like our previous ones did.

We've learned that we all have created the relationships we have.

And, if you want something new, whether it's in the relationship you're in or the one you want to be in, you're the one who's going to create it.

You're going to create it from who you are BEING.

If you're love, you're going to create from that.

If you're creating from a place of possibilities, you're going to create that.

If you're creating from past beliefs you've dragged along and called "reality," then you're going to create from that.

If you're creating your relationships from fear, distance, separation and doubt, you're going to create that in your real life.

If all of your relationships really are a "creation" (and they are), then you get to decide how you're going to create them.

What do you want them to look like?

How deep do you want your connection to be?

How alive, rich and growing do you want your love?

It all starts with the next thought you choose to believe and the choice about what desire you want to make real.

Have fun with this.

You are the creator.

You get to choose.

Will the other person always cooperate and act like you want them to?

Of course not, but you get to choose whether you react with love or with actions or words that separate the two of you.

While not everyone is going to have a soul mate experience like ours, everyone, including you, can have much more love in their lives than they do right now.

"When you stop expecting people to be perfect, you can like them for who they are."

Donald Miller

Chapter 8
The Possibilities of an Undefended Heart By Susie

Defend. Defend. Defend.

It's so easy to get defensive when someone, especially a loved one, thinks or acts differently from what you think is "right."

It just seems natural or "healthy" to defend a belief and make the other person "see the light."

Or in other words, make the other person wrong when you have a difference of opinion.

In some weird way, we humans believe this automatic defensive attitude will get us what we want.

But it never does. It just creates separation, distance and misunderstanding.

I remember times in the early days our relationship, automatically lashing out at Otto because of his "belittling" tone of voice, especially when I couldn't figure out some computer issue when I'd asked him for help.

I'd become defensive and then Otto would become defensive and angry.

Sound familiar?

After all, he didn't understand what my problem was.

He thought he was just trying to help and was unaware of the meaning I attached to his tone and words.

In fact, he was unaware that he even had a belittling tone of voice at all!

If you stand back and look closely at what's going on during times like these like we finally did,

You can see that when your heart closes, you build walls and any possibility of connection, love and understanding evaporates.

When connection, love and understanding become more important than believing your story about the other person that you've made up,

When you see that defensiveness only creates defensiveness from the other person, along with arguments and shutting down,

You can choose what we're calling an "undefended heart" and that means choosing to respond with love rather than reacting and defending your "rightness."

And you can choose it moment by moment.

When I saw that my defensiveness only stirred up defensiveness and anger in Otto, I made the choice to shift out of the "story" I'd made up to make sense of his actions.

When I did that, I saw that the meaning I'd put on Otto's tone of voice was that he thought I was stupid because I couldn't figure out the computer problem.

I also realized this was often how I'd felt with my father—stupid—which came up when I was growing up and trying to help him with building or fix-it projects or failing miserably at something he thought I should already know how to do.

I truthfully doubt he thought I was stupid, but somehow I got the idea that I wasn't pleasing him in some situations.

When I told Otto my discovery, he softened and he revealed that his "tone" could have come from his uncertainty that he could fix the computer issue.

His "tone" was nothing about me but rather more about his insecurities.

I'd been defending against the fears and old beliefs inside me that said I really was stupid, but it was nothing that was real.

This was a powerful lesson for us and showed us both the possibilities for love of an undefended heart.

We all have different ways of seeing the world, mainly from past experiences that create different beliefs.

Differences are just a given in relationships, especially with those closest to us, and they can be gifts.

When these differences blindside you, it's so easy to fall into defensiveness, thinking you have to stand up for yourself.

But when you see there's nothing to defend and that defensiveness doesn't get you what you want anyway, you can choose to listen to what's inside you and to the other person for understanding and for possibilities instead of arguing.

Ask for more information if you don't understand and then listen.

When you're open and curious about why the person thinks and feels the way they do, it's usually nothing even close to what you dreamed up and assigned to them. Slow down, stay open and learn.

Know that you have a choice and you don't have to agree to anything that you really are against doing. Relax into that knowing.

Neither person has to "give up" who they are but when you understand where the other person is coming from, there's more compassion and understanding in your daily life.

Consider the idea that you might learn something from this person about this issue. Open yourself to seeing it from a little different perspective.

When you do, you'll be able to experience the beauty, the gifts and the many miracles that can come to you in a relationship when you live with an undefended heart.

What if you think there really is something to defend?

You can become aware of the feelings inside that come up from the thought that you must defend your point of view.

Then ask yourself if defending will get you what you want or not.

Or will an open, undefended heart filled with possibilities that can include a loving boundary and request be what's called for instead?

The choice is always yours.

Chapter 9
Five Magic Words

The next time you're tempted to give someone your unsolicited opinion or advice, why not use these "Magic Words" to keep both of your hearts open and invite them to some new possibilities?

Ask them a question like this:

"Would you be open to_____?"

And then, fill in the blank with an invitation for them to hear what you see or think about this situation and then wait for their response.

You might even ask one of these questions:

"Would you be open to some feedback about that?"

"Would you be open to some other ways to see this situation?"

Or

"Would you be open to some unsolicited advice about that?"

And again, the key is to truly be an invitation here and not a bully who has to make them see something the way you see it.

If you do this, what you'll find is that sometimes other people are open to your advice, opinions or suggestions and sometimes they're not.

By using these words as a sentence starter and "asking" whether they want your input instead of forcing them to hear your advice or opinion when they didn't ask for it, it will do two things:

It will allow you to offer them a gift of love in the form of an "invitation" to a new possibility if they choose to accept it.

It will let them know they are respected and they do have a choice whether to open to hearing your advice or not. And you're good with it either way.

If they choose not to open to hearing your advice or opinion, it will also let them know you value their "inner wisdom" and honor how they choose to see a situation or move forward even if you don't agree with it.

This can be tough sometimes, but using words like those we shared above and "asking" instead of telling can make all the difference between whether they keep their heart open to you or not.

It can also make a huge difference in the quality of your connection.

Make a request and not a demand and then listen and honor the other person's answer.

You'll be amazed at the willingness of the other person to keep their heart open and actually listen when you do this.

Chapter 10
Your Buts are the Problem

One of the things that triggers a person to start a new exercise program (usually around January 1ˢᵗ) is when they start to notice "Hey, my butt is getting a little too big here and I need to do something."

And one of the places that keeps a person from giving and getting all the love they want is when their "buts" are too big.

We're talking about different kinds of "buts" here and the truth is anytime you make your "buts" important, your possibilities for love shrink when they don't have to.

In a way, it's like you're using the word "but" as a qualifier for how much you are going to argue for a limitation of why you can't have, be or do something.

Over the years, we've had hundreds of people say to us things like this:

- "I'd be kinder to him but he doesn't deserve it."
- "I'd listen to her more of the time but she's so irritating."

- "I'd spend time with my partner but I'm so busy doing other things I have to do."

- "I'd like to have a partner but all the good ones are taken."

What if you just got rid of everything that comes after the "but"?

What if you just made a declaration and said,

"I'm going to be kinder."

"I'm going to listen to what they have to say more."

Or

"I'd like to have a partner" instead of putting a qualifier on it.

Here's the important truth for you to take in:

The words you use when you talk to yourself (or to anyone else) matter.

The words you use either create possibilities or shut them down.

When it comes to your "buts,"

What comes before the "but" could be what you truly want or possibly wanted in the past but aren't allowing yourself to want in the present moment simply because of the "but" that you're allowing to get in the way.

Whatever comes after the "but" limits your possibilities, shrinks down your chances of having what you want and may not be true.

Here's an example of how this can play out in real life.

Recently a woman named Ellen asked us this:

"I'd love to have the kind of BIG FAT LOVE you're talking about in this book but how do you stay open and loving when so many other obligations and responsibilities seem to get in the way?"

She also wanted to know, "How do you have the time (and mostly the energy) to create and cultivate a truly special love relationship when you've got the demands of children, crazy work schedules, sleep deprivation and limited child-free time?"

As we think about her questions and concerns, it occurs to us that her experience could be so much different by switching the words she's using to more of what she wants instead of what she doesn't want.

She's using the word "but" instead of "and."

When you use the word "but," it's a full stop.

It's also bringing to life a thought you believe that says, "I could have, do or be THIS but _____" and then you fill in the blank with your perceived limitation.

Instead you can use the word "and" and look for solutions or possibilities for how you could have, be or do something rather than how you can't.

The word "and" invites fresh new possibilities and the word "but" reveals where you are putting the brakes on possibility thinking.

Consider the huge difference in possibilities (and results) on the other side of these two sentences immediately below and ask yourself which has the feeling of more possibilities?

"I could have much more love in my life but with all the constant demands I'm under with my young children, there's just not enough time (or me) to go around."

Or

"How could I give my children everything they need AND have BIG FAT LOVE with my partner, too?"

We think the sentence with more possibilities is obvious and the possibilities could include brain-storming with her partner about other child-care or home chore options and ways to carve out even a small amount of time to be together.

Think about it.

When do you use the word "but"?

How often?

And specifically, what are your "buts" that limit you and stop you from having what you want?

It might even be helpful to make a running list of them as they come up.

Whatever your "buts" are, notice them, acknowledge them and then let them go if you don't want your possibilities to shrink.

Whatever comes before your "buts" is almost always what you want when you don't put any limitation on it.

Placing your focus and attention on what you want is where the magic is in creating the love and life you want.

Using the word "and" helps you see more and open to more love and possibilities.

Your "buts" only get in the way of that.

"Do the best you can until you know better. Then when you know better, do better."

Maya Angelou

Chapter 11
No Failures

Before the two of us got together, Otto was married to someone else for 15 years and Susie was married to someone else for 30 years.

Both of those marriages ended in divorce and some people would call those relationships failures.

But, we've come to see it differently.

What if there was no such thing as failure in love?

What if your past experiences in your love relationships up until now were simply "learning opportunities" for creating something new, fresh and amazing?

Most people don't see their "failures" at love or in any other part of their lives as learning opportunities because they're not asking themselves the right kind of questions.

If love seems to be a struggle, you might be asking yourself disempowering questions like these:

"Why didn't he want me?", "Why am I such a failure at love?" or "Why am I so bad at choosing a partner?"

And of course, "Why are relationships so hard?"

If you want to see new possibilities for love in your life, practice asking yourself questions that open you to seeing life in ways that create more of what you want.

A question like, "What can I learn from this situation that will help me create more loving relationships?" will do wonders for creating something special now or in the future.

Even though Susie's first marriage ended in divorce and could be considered a failure, she saw it as a gift. It not only produced their beautiful daughter, but also this marriage had provided her the freedom to explore a myriad of self-growth topics that she might not have had otherwise.

What she learned in these explorations has helped her become who she is today.

When you're able to move beyond blaming yourself or the other person and instead look at what you learned, you'll create a happier, healthier life.

The truth is that there really is no such thing as a failure at love. There are only the ways you choose to see what is happening in the moment or what happened before.

You get to choose what you're going to create with your thinking about love.

Not your friends, your neighbors or anyone else in your life.

Only you.

"What you focus
on expands."

Otto Collins

Chapter 12
Finger-Pointing

A coaching client (we'll call her Sally) realized that although sometimes it felt good for a moment to lash out and criticize her husband's anger, the hour-long argument that usually ensued between the two of them as she defended how "right" she was didn't feel good.

After a while, she began to see that underneath her criticism of her husband was a deep frustration with how everything seemed out of control.

And he wasn't at fault for all of what she perceived was wrong in her life.

When Sally saw that, she realized that fighting and blaming him really wasn't solving anything and was actually hurting her marriage.

And she could make another choice.

When you're focusing on what's wrong in your life, you're constantly reinforcing and upping the stress you're carrying, making it easy to blame others.

There's no room for anything new to show itself.

When you're in the thick of blaming each other, it's so difficult to see it and do anything differently.

We've found that becoming aware BEFORE you're in it is the key to moving into more love and understanding.

Like Sally, you can choose to look in a different direction if you're caught in a damaging, blaming cycle.

You might consider slowing down and asking yourself questions like these:

"How am I contributing to this?" and "How can I see this differently?"

When you ask yourself questions like these and you're open to the answers that come from them, you'll be able to see that blaming yourself or the other person doesn't take you toward what you want.

You'll be able to see a kinder, more loving way of being with yourself and with this other person.

Love and ease can follow and that finger-pointing loop disappears.

If you want Big Fat Love, become aware of the cost of the blame you may be entangled in.

Become aware of the possibilities of love that can be created when you give yourself permission to move out of that loop.

Focus on What Can Go Right

Like Sally, a lot of us spend our mental energy focusing on what's wrong now or what could possibly go wrong in the future.

What if you flipped that around and just decided to only focus on what could go right?

What if all the things you focused on or worried about never happened and your love just kept getting better and better?

This is the beauty and magic of focusing on what's right instead of what's wrong and what you don't want to happen.

We've heard it said many times over the years that what you focus on in your life expands.

And we've found it to be true more times than we could count.

In the last year or so, Otto's been referring to Susie as the "Incredible Susie."

He's been intentionally doing this both when he talks to her and when he's talking about her to someone else.

He's been doing this because it brings more attention inside him to what he wants to focus on and claim. It also crowds out negativity that can pop up about her that he certainly doesn't want to expand.

Here's something worth considering:

What if you consciously decided right now to focus only on either what's right or what could go right in all of your relationships?

If you decided to do that, your possibilities for love would multiply many times over.

And THAT is something worth focusing on.

"To see a new reality, you must choose a new belief that supports that reality."

Townsend Wardlaw

Chapter 13
Jumping Out of the Known

The possibilities in love and life are always hidden in the unknown.

And the unknown is nothing more or less than the place you may not yet be able to see in this moment.

If you want to create new possibilities in your life, we invite you to stop seeing it the way you've always seen it. Look past what you already know and open to a new direction.

When you try to create something new but are coming from the place of familiarity and the same beliefs and actions you've been accustomed to believing and doing,

You just keep creating the same outcomes over and over and wonder why it's not getting you what you want.

When you give yourself permission to step out of what you already know, you're inviting something new and fresh to come in.

And what's new and fresh is in the unknown.

Always.

When you're living from the unknown, you may feel a bit like a novice trapeze artist, letting go of one trapeze bar to grab onto the other one swinging in the breeze.

You may not know what's next or the best option yet and you may have plenty of fears, doubts and concerns about a new road or path.

And that's okay.

As Napoleon Hill, author of the self-help classic book *Think and Grow Rich* once said, "Just go as far as you can see and when you get there, you will be able to see even farther."

When you rest in the calm space within your mind and heart called your "inner knowing," you'll always be guided and know what step to take next.

And maybe you don't need to know what's beyond that!

This is because that's the place where faith, trust and possibilities intersect.

This willingness to venture into the unknown is the key to opening to new possibilities.

The Seat of Uncomfortability

Being uncomfortable often goes right along with jumping into the unknown.

The willingness to be uncomfortable a little bit (or maybe a lot) in order to create the love that you want may be a requirement if you're going to give and receive all that is possible for you in this lifetime.

Like most of us, you can feel uncomfortable in difficult moments when there's a struggle between opening your heart to someone and closing it.

You can see the uncomfortable feeling as a warning sign to pull back.

But there's another possibility here.

You can choose to see discomfort not as something to avoid or defend against but as a sign that you are coming up against a belief that's trying to get your attention, to be acknowledged and maybe let go of.

Our experience says that there is great freedom on the other side of letting go of a belief that no longer serves you.

And you get to decide!

If there is discomfort, then you can know that you're holding onto something that is keeping you stuck at a certain level of loving and living.

You don't have to stay stuck.

You can choose to see any discomfort that smacks you in the face as a sign and a gift that something important is ready to be let go of so you can see, feel and have more of the love you want in your life.

Discomfort is a gift if you choose to see it that way.

You can always create something new if you're willing to open to being uncomfortable as you step into the unknown.

"Keeping things inside does not make them any better. When you do not open up, you set yourself up to blow up."

Iyanla Vanzant

Chapter 14
Saying What's Scary

What would you like to say to your partner, a friend or a family member but are scared to?

Whatever that is—and don't tell us that there's nothing—is the thing that very often must be said.

The reason that thing must be said is because that's where the freedom is.

This is also where the possibility of a deeper connection resides.

The freedom that we're talking about here is the freedom to share what you've been holding back that interferes with your connection with this person.

Yes, we know and agree that it's not a good idea to open up and start baring your soul to someone you don't trust or in a situation that could be damaging or hurt you in some way.

We also don't recommend that you engage in something we call "verbal vomiting," where you're just spewing hate or harsh words at someone or are trying to hurt them in a way they don't deserve.

And still

Sometimes saying the thing that must be shared is a non-negotiable, full bodied "Yes, I have to share this or I won't be able to feel complete about this subject, topic or situation."

Saying what's scary isn't necessarily about the other person and it isn't about "confronting" someone about something.

It's also not about gathering the courage to tell someone off or make them wrong.

Although, there will be times when what you'll share may be difficult for someone else to hear or take in, saying what's scary is more about speaking your truth, practicing emotional honesty and creating a deeper connection rather than "letting them have it."

If something has been gnawing at you and interfering with the relationship you want, it could be time to say what's true for you with love and without blame or confrontation.

When you open to inviting a heartfelt, honest discussion, you're not confronting anyone with your truth or your fears.

You're simply sharing and a lot can come from that if you're open to it.

If you're saying what's scary, there's a certain vulnerability that's going to be present and that can invite vulnerability and openness from that other person as well.

In other words, you're sharing about you and you're listening from a loving space inside you, inviting them to do the same.

You're creating the space for an opening to deeper love.

We'll have more to say about vulnerability in an upcoming chapter, but consider this:

By saying what's scary, you could also be opening the doorway to your relationship changing in a more wonderful way.

On the other side of saying the thing you fear from the most loving place your heart has to offer is a true, rich aliveness and emotional honesty that is rare in most relationships.

New possibilities exist and are created in the space where fear meets "I have to share this or I won't be allowing my heart to open to full blossom."

We're talking about sharing the thing in a loving conversation that feels like it's coming from deep inside and that must be shared in service to connection.

This "sharing in service to connection" is the important part.

This is because the people in your life want the full you and not the fear-ridden, half full version of you.

Give them that.

Give them all of you.

That's what the people in your life crave.

ALL of You!

Give them all of that and watch your love and the possibilities with those people expand greatly.

"The only person you need to believe in you... Is you."

Otto Collins

Chapter 15
Say "Yes" to You

As we were writing this chapter, Otto was instantly transported back in time to a moment when he literally beat himself up.

As he recalls, he was 12 or 13 years old, walking down a road that led to the railroad tracks and a field near the river where he'd go for solitude when all of a sudden, he was overcome by intense pain, judgment, anger and self-loathing.

He was so overwhelmed with these feelings that he actually took his fist and punched himself in the face two or three times so hard that he busted his lip and hurt his jaw.

When he got home, his mother asked what happened, and rather than admit the truth, which was that his hatred of himself and his story of his life in that moment got the best of him, he simply told her a lie—which was that he fell and hurt himself.

There are going to be moments in every person's life, like the moment in Otto's life we just described, when you don't like yourself or your life, you don't think you're worthy of love or you don't see how more love is possible for you.

And yet

What we're calling saying "yes" to you is critical to expanding your possibilities for love and the success of any relationship.

On a practical level, here's what we think it is:

- It might mean saying "yes" to an invitation you want to accept even though someone in your life may not think it's a good idea.

- It might mean asking for help when you haven't in the past.

- It might mean supporting yourself with a much-needed nap.

- It might mean being your own advocate with medical personnel.

- It might mean saying "no" to going to an event you're really not interested in instead of saying "yes" and attending with resentment or trying to get out of going at the last minute.

- Saying "yes" to you might mean being willing to ask for what you want.

- It could mean deciding you're not willing to settle for less than the best and highest vision you can dream up for love.

- It can mean committing to more fun, deeper connection and more passion, not just in your relationship but in your whole life.

- Saying "yes" to you might mean not believing limiting thoughts about yourself.

- Saying "yes" to you might mean following your intuition even when logic might suggest otherwise.

- Saying "yes" to you might mean YOU being your best advocate even though you may not be able to see your awesomeness.

- Saying "yes" to you might mean saying "yes" to him or her or it might mean a big fat "no."
- We could go on and on with examples but the bottom line is this —

Saying "yes" to you is the ultimate expression of self-love.

Self-love starts with deep listening to what's truly inside you, coupled with the intention to create connected relationships and a loving life.

The amount of self-love you have is a way to play small or a way to show up as the divine gift that we were born to be.

It's the opportunity of a lifetime to say "yes" and embrace the oneness of all that is within the mind, heart and soul chosen to come forth right here, right now at this time to be the ultimate expression of our Creator's love and gift to us all.

Or it's the rejection of our very essence.

Chapter 16
When It's All Give and No Get

Marcia was one of our relationship coaching clients a few years back and the pain of her 15 year marriage was obvious and palpable.

During our first "get-to-know-you" conversation, Marcia was so shaken, so upset and crying "snot-tears" to such a degree that all we could do in that moment was to be with her.

She was alternating between fear, anger and downright hostility and finally calmed down enough that we could talk with her.

She shared that she didn't know how much longer she could hold on if this was what love and life with her husband, who she called "Big Chuck," was going to be like forever.

And then, just as quickly as she had calmed down, her anger and fear heated up again and she just started screaming the following words:

"I give everything and he gives NOTHING! All I want is for him to love me the way I love him and he just won't or maybe he can't or it's just not possible for him to love me back the way I wish he would."

When she finally managed to calm down again, we asked her how this made her feel.

To this, she simply replied, "I feel alone, afraid and rejected."

At this point, you may be wondering what a story like this is doing in a book about BIG FAT LOVE and more possibilities.

And to that we will say EVERYTHING.

And here's why.

Whether you realize it or not, when it comes to love, you, Marcia and us are all exactly alike in one respect.

We all have the choice to open our hearts, minds and souls as love in this (and every) moment regardless of the circumstances.

It's totally true.

In this moment, you may be kind to someone and they may not choose to respond with kindness.

You may be loving and they may not choose to respond with love.

You may choose to be vulnerable in this moment with someone and they may choose to remain distant, aloof or armored up.

You may want to have more intimacy or romance in your relationship and the other person may not seem interested.

You may bend over backwards or do way more than you're paid to do at work and your boss or others may not see this, appreciate it or celebrate it or you.

These and many other things that don't feel good are very real possibilities.

However, the fact remains, in every moment you have a choice about whether to open as love and stay open to the possibilities of love or not.

You also have a choice about whether to see yourself as a victim or not.

To see a bright future for yourself or not.

To look at the reality of your life and your present circumstances or to allow your "stinking thinking" (any thoughts that take you away from what you want) to suffocate your possibilities.

To focus on the good, the positive and what's working instead of all the aspects of the relationship that you aren't happy with.

But what if you continue to love, continue to stay open and give all you have to give to them and he or she really isn't giving you anything in return?

What do you do then?

Assuming you want to increase your possibilities for love with the person you're with (or the person you want to be with), continue to open your heart, mind and soul.

Not so easy when you don't get anything in return, right?

Instead of giving up, you can ask yourself new questions (or get the help of a good coach) to help you see some new possibilities you may be having trouble seeing.

Some questions you may want to ask yourself to stimulate more possibilities for Big Fat Love in your life could include (but aren't limited to) these:

- What do I really want here?
- What am I committed to?
- If I was willing to, what could I see differently about this other person or this situation that could change everything or improve anything?
- Am I open to new possibilities or am I shut down?

- What have I NOT been willing to do to open the door to more possibilities here?
- Am I looking for good about this person or this situation or am I mostly focused on what's not working or what's painful?
- Have I tried a thousand different things or have I tried the same approach (to get a different result) a thousand times?

But what if you realize that you really have had it?

Whether it's a marriage, an intimate relationship, a friendship or some other kind of relationship,

What if there's no more fire for the relationship?

What if you're done trying and you really do want to call it quits?

If that's the case, we encourage you to ask yourself this question:

What is the kindest and most loving thing I can do for myself and everyone else involved here?

It might be to keep trying or it might mean the relationship needs to end.

Whatever your best answer to this question is, it will probably involve some if not all of the following:

- The willingness to be honest both with yourself and the other people in the relationship.
- Authenticity and being authentic to the truth.
- The willingness to be vulnerable and showing up as love without fear no matter what you decide.

As we wind up this chapter, here's one last thought about what it might take to start creating some new possibilities around love.

Most of the time, people will only allow themselves to be truly vulnerable when they feel like they have nothing left to lose.

Otto recalls the final days of his first marriage (after he completely decided to leave).

"In those final days of being together and living under the same roof, there were times when my ex and I were more vulnerable with each other and said things to each other in ways that were more open, more candid, and more truthful than we possibly ever had."

In this situation, it was "too little, too late."

But it does bring an interesting question to mind.

What if you decided that being vulnerable and speaking the kind truth and allowing that other person to do the same is more important than holding onto any fears, doubts, hurts or mistakes either of you may have made?

What if you saw you could do this BEFORE the relationship had to end instead of after?

Maybe, just maybe, if you did this,

More miracles and love may be possible for you with this person or in this situation than you might think.

"The way you can know how much you're attached to any story is how much you hold back. When you hold back, you feel it. It's not comfortable."

Byron Katie

Chapter 17
Vulnerability is a Superpower

Of all the things that create a deeper love and a true heart-felt connection with another human, "vulnerability" is on the short list every single time.

And yet

We hold back.

We hesitate to give all of ourselves.

And more often than not, we're not enough of a safe space for others to truly open to us.

So, why is vulnerability so important and how vulnerable should you be?

When you hold back, don't open your heart and don't trust, the other people in your life feel it.

They can't feel the "real" you!

Unless you truly fear for your physical or emotional safety, vulnerability isn't the place to hold back if you want more love and a closer connection with another human.

You get to decide how vulnerable you want to be by how committed you are to more love.

That's how it works.

When you're willing to take a chance and reveal things you may not want to admit even to yourself, you're vulnerable.

There is power in vulnerability.

Early in our relationship, Susie saw how she'd been keeping others, even those she loved, at arm's length when she'd say she was "fine" and she really wasn't.

She saw that her persona of "Miss Having-It-All-Together" and not asking for help created distance between her and others.

When she was honest about what she was feeling without pointing a blaming finger outward, she came to see how being vulnerable could disarm defensiveness and open heart-felt conversations.

The fact that there is power in allowing yourself to BE vulnerable has been a tough one for us as well as for many of our coaching clients.

Maybe it is for you.

And yet

What we have found in our own relationship and in the relationships of our coaching clients that really feel close and connected is this:

Sometimes, the thing that you feel can't be said, shouldn't be said and the thing you fear saying is the thing that MUST be said.

Not out of some weird desire for drama and the desire to feel like you should "be free to say ANYTHING."

No, it's the fact that when you are willing to share the thing you fear to share, the people in your life feel you more deeply. When you do this, it makes them want more of THAT and not the "you" that holds back.

We understand about the fears that vulnerability brings up because we used to think that being vulnerable was to be feared, to be held back, a weakness and not to be accepted in ourselves and others.

After all, isn't it a sign of weakness if you allow yourself to let the world see who you really are, flaws and all?

You don't want to "hurt" the other person with your truth, right?

We used to think like this and now we know this is a story that will keep your love at arms-length, your connection lacking and your possibilities small.

Sharing your truth with love can be more powerful than you realize for both you and the other person.

But, what about the flip side of this question?

How much vulnerability should you expect from others?

The answer is simple.

None.

They will allow themselves to be as vulnerable as they allow themselves to be.

Part of this is how safe they feel with you.

The other part of this has nothing whatsoever to do with you.

You can't force someone else to be vulnerable or open to you.

You can only experience vulnerability from others when they show up as vulnerable and not a minute before.

It's important not to make up any stories and create expectations about the other person and their potential for vulnerability.

If you constantly say to yourself something like this,

"He (or she or they) will never let me in and be honest with me so why should I be!"

You may miss an opening that could lead to a loving, honest conversation.

Instead, keep opening, opening, opening and see what happens.

The other person will open to you more and more in their own timing and in their own way if they don't feel pushed or forced to reveal themselves in ways they're not willing to in that moment.

They will be vulnerable with you when they feel they can be vulnerable with you.

Not a minute before and not a minute later.

Vulnerability is a Superpower

It opens closed hearts, it opens closed minds and it opens doors of possibilities that weren't able to be opened before.

How much someone else is willing to be vulnerable with you may have nothing to do with you or it may have everything to do with you.

The biggest thing you can do to invite the people in your life to show up with more vulnerability is for YOU to show up with more vulnerability mixed with love and acceptance. That's all.

Chapter 18

Boundaries That Make Love Stronger

Here's a question for you.

Are your boundaries soft, weak and pliable like liquid, hard and solid like a rock or somewhere in-between?

The truth is that everyone has boundaries whether they know what they are or not.

The problem is that, with most people, their boundaries don't actually make love stronger.

In many cases, they actually do the opposite. They keep you from enjoying the depth and abundance of love that is possible for you.

It's time to see "boundaries" in a whole new way.

A way that eliminates "battle lines" and still has you creating the love and connection you want and need while still being true to you.

Here's the way setting a boundary usually goes:

Something happens or maybe a LOT of things happen that are unacceptable for you. You decide you're not going to take any more or you're not going to accept what's going on any more and you decide—this is it, THIS has to change or else.

You steel yourself to have "the talk," you put a hard, protective shell around yourself and put up your defenses.

You may or may not be clear and second guess yourself, questioning whether you're being unreasonable, too emotional, not loving or any other self-judgment that occurs to you.

You may not know where or how to draw that line or what you'll do if the other person doesn't honor the boundary and crosses it.

The other person can get defensive, shut down and may lie to you and agree to something they have no intention to follow through with. They may start an argument.

There could be no real agreement even though you think and hope there is one.

But there's a way to lovingly approach expressing what's true for you that can make love stronger and bring you closer.

This starts in your own mind with two words, "Yes…and."

"Yes, this is what's true for me and…"

"Yes, this is a NO for me at this time and…"

Or

"Yes, this is a deal-breaker for me and…"

"And" helps you stay open to the possibility that you both may shift to see something new.

Having flexibility doesn't mean giving up your values but it does mean that what you thought might not be completely true.

And it may mean that there's an opportunity for a resolution to the issue to emerge that you hadn't seen yet.

Sometimes your boundary is a deal breaker for you and you need to know that for yourself.

Again, this will come from a deep knowing inside you.

From that knowing, you'll know where or if to draw a line.

The truth is all of this can be done with love instead of hardness and anger.

The truth is that your boundary can change in time.

A friend, who is in her 60s, recently told us that her new boyfriend was moving in with her and started to talk about "getting married" way too early for her to consider.

After a discussion with him, she was able to set some healthy boundaries around marriage and money that were true for her in this moment.

And she was wise enough to know that those boundaries could change but for now, she knew this was how she could move deeper into their relationship while loving herself and continuing to love him.

A boundary can certainly be healthy for you and for the other person if it comes from truth and honesty and not from rigidness and fear.

We started this chapter with the possibility that you can actually create boundaries that make love stronger (and you can).

If you're someone whose go-to method of creating a boundary is always something akin to a concrete wall with a stop sign on the front of it, then your boundary is probably being met with resistance and may or may not be honored.

Making love stronger won't be possible with JUST the feeling of a concrete wall behind the boundary.

To create boundaries that make love stronger, here are a few things you might want to try:

- Continuing to love that other person in spite of your differences
- Being clear about what's a "deal breaker" for you and what isn't
- Watching your language. In other words, choosing your words wisely. Some words connect and others divide. Always choose words that connect instead of divide. And finally
- Approaching the boundaries you feel need to be created from a place of possibility of deepening love instead of impossibility.

At this point, you may be wondering something like this:

Will there be times when this keep-your-heart-open-while-having boundaries idea just won't work? Will there be times when you just have to draw a line in the sand and be clear that the line isn't to be crossed NO MATTER WHAT?

Are there going to be times when you have to put on your full armor and go into full protection mode so your boundaries will be honored?

To this, we say, yes, there may be times like this but not as often as you think.

If the goal is always to increase love and connection between you and another, staying open instead of shutting down is always a better strategy.

"Always be kinder than you think you need to be."

Otto Collins

Chapter 19
The Power of Acknowledgement

It was only a moment in time but it was one that showed us how important acknowledgement really was and the gift that something as small and easy as a smile and a wave could be.

The two of us frequently take walks together in our neighborhood, always waving and saying hello to those who are sitting on their porches or walking their dogs.

Christian, a neighbor who had recently moved from Kenya, always returned our greetings and seemed happy to see us.

We had no idea that our show of love for each other by holding hands as we walked, as well as our warmly acknowledging him, impacted him until one summer evening a few years ago.

Here's what happened after he rushed to the sidewalk from his porch chair to talk with us:

"How do you do it?" Christian asked after hearing us tell him we had been married nearly 25 years, were about to have our wedding anniversary and were obviously still in love.

"How do you stay in love for 20 or 25 years when I'm struggling to make it to 10 years?"

As we talked about how we stay in love, we told him how important acknowledgement was to keeping a relationship healthy and that this moment is the only moment you have to do that.

If you treat that other person like THIS moment is the only one and the last one you'll ever have together and also express it,

Special moments will be created and before long, you'll have a lifetime of special moments because you don't take each other for granted.

Christian had never thought of this and could see the truth of it.

He could see how our acknowledgement of him each time we walked by, (which not everyone did), showed him warmth and love.

He also saw how this could serve as an example for how he could treat his wife with more presence, love and appreciation.

In every moment in every relationship, there's a choice and a chance for true connection.

You either open your heart and accept the risk of acting and speaking from love or you close your heart, separating yourself from another.

You either acknowledge and appreciate when that other person has done something for you or has shown you kindness or you let that opportunity for love pass by forever.

Whether it's a stranger or someone close to you, you LOSE the opportunity to meet another in love in that moment.

When Otto's father was alive and he would hear of someone physically not doing well or he'd be in a reflective mood after someone he cared about died, he would say,

"I want my flowers while I'm living."

Otto's dad wanted to be acknowledged, appreciated and loved while he was living and cautioned Otto to not wait until he was no longer in physical form to express it.

This is such great advice for keeping any relationship healthy and strong.

There is power in acknowledgement and there's great love that's available for all who see and express it as well as receive it.

Imagine the possibilities if you consciously and deliberately decided to become the king or queen of acknowledgement.

Imagine how it would open the hearts of the people closest to you if you gave them true, honest and sincere appreciation on a more regular basis.

Would their hearts be open or closed to you more of the time?

Would they see the best in you more of the time instead of the worst?

Would they start looking for the good in you and acknowledging you more of the time?

We're guessing the answer would be yes, yes and yes.

We're not suggesting that you go through your day and make up stuff that isn't true, isn't real or isn't genuine to acknowledge people for. We also don't advise that you give acknowledgement to get it back.

That can always backfire on you and lead to disappointment if you don't get what you expect to get back.

What we know to be true is that when you start looking in the direction of appreciating someone, you'll see more to appreciate about them and more to appreciate in your life.

And THAT will open the doorway to more possibilities for more and deeper love.

Chapter 20
Taming the Monsters in Your Head

Call them "monsters" or whatever you want.

There are voices saying things to you in your own head almost all the time.

Perhaps you've noticed.

It's like these voices inside your head are narrating a running monologue (that only you can hear) describing and judging what they see is going on in YOUR life.

Most of the time these voices are commenting about you, criticizing you, telling you what you should or should not be doing and how you're not good enough.

These voices in your head are judging the other people in your life, too.

Usually, these voices in your head are talking about you and everything and everyone else who shows up in your life in ways that aren't kind, helpful, positive, loving, supportive, or self-esteem boosting.

And in almost every case, what those voices have to say simply isn't true.

In fact, just like the "monsters" that lived under your bed when you were a kid had no substance when the lights were turned on—

The "monster" voices in your head almost always have no substance either.

We found this out when the two of us were first together.

The "monsters in our heads" started bringing up fears and made us believe the love we had just discovered wouldn't last.

They jabbered about what our 16-year age difference could mean and made us doubt whether we should even continue with the relationship.

Because of this, Susie was afraid that Otto wouldn't find her attractive as she aged and Otto was afraid that he would lose her too early when he was still young.

The good news is that we both made the choice to ignore those voices in our heads, bypass our fears and go for love because we realized we're never promised any moment except the one we're living in right now.

We chose to stay in and enjoy the present moment because the truth is that no one knows the future.

Here's what we've seen:

If you listen to and believe what those voices in your head say to you, most of the time, it will not help you see the good in yourself or the good in others.

If you take what these voices say seriously, they will crush your willingness and ability to open to new possibilities for love in your life.

The only voice worth listening to is the voice of truth.

And that voice is the one that says that you are a soul and a being of light and love.

That voice of truth is the voice that reminds you that you have come here on this planet full of love.

The voice of truth will remind you of the good, the pure and the beautiful in others and in yourself.

It will remind you why you love another, why you chose to be with them, why you choose to spend time with them and why you care for them.

The voice of truth will remind you that you are made from love and your mission here is to show up in ways that automatically allow you to experience and to create even more love in this lifetime.

Anything other than that is just your fears and your ego talking, trying to convince you of who you are not.

"Everything you've ever
done has led you to
THIS moment.
Don't let anything
distract you from it!"

From the film
"Everything Everywhere All At Once"

Chapter 21

All In

Many people make such a big deal over the idea of being "all in."

"All in" in a relationship

"All in" in a life

"All in" in a business

But what if the only thing you needed to be "all in" on is this moment?

You can pick your word.

"All in" for passion

"All in" for commitment

"All in" for your partner

"All in" for you

"All in" for healing the darkness of your fearful heart

"All in" for kindness

"All in" for seeing only the good in your beloved and others

"All in" for loving touch

You get to choose which possibility you want.

"All in" always and only happens in this present moment.

Not some kind of commitment to tomorrow or next week or forever.

Not from some kind of commitment based on fear, "shoulds" or "have to's."

Try creating your possibilities in love and life from a new, different kind of "all in."

The kind of "all in" that touches the soul, speaks to the heart and loves from the deepest place imaginable.

That's the best kind of "all in."

"You're not really over it if you're still talking about it."

Abraham-Hicks

Chapter 22
When to Hold onto Grudges

Otto knows how destructive holding onto a grudge is to love and connection.

He knows this because he carried one against his father for 38 years until a few short years ago when he wrote *Preaching to Monkeys: Hope, Healing, and Understanding for Fathers, Sons, and the People Who Love Them.*

One of the stories in the book is about a painful time in his childhood when his father abruptly decided to sell the nicest house Otto's family had ever lived in while he was growing up. Otto was upset because he was taken away from his best friends and a school he liked with no explanation.

Otto made up a story about why all of this happened and he thought it was because of Mrs. Daubs.

Mrs. Daubs, the woman who lived next door, was mean as a snake and 12-year-old Otto thought she needed to be treated as such. He'd throw rocks at her dogs and bust glass bottles on her porch as he walked by.

As a payback, she'd spray Otto's father with her hose and cuss at him at 11pm at night when he got off work. Otto had made up a story that his father had let this woman's meanness drive them from their home and out of the neighborhood.

Every time he thought about this, he saw his father as a coward, a wimp or a pushover for allowing her to do this and he held a grudge because of it.

It wasn't until his father had passed and he was researching and verifying the stories he wanted to put in *Preaching to Monkeys* that he asked his mother why they moved.

She told him that his father loved him so much that he wanted to protect him from Mrs. Daubs. Otto didn't know this but she had accused him of trying to kill her dogs and poison her hedges (which he didn't do) and his father was afraid she'd hurt Otto in some way.

For nearly 40 years, Otto thought they moved because his father was weak, letting that woman get the best of him.

When Otto found out the truth, he was able to instantly let go of all of that judgment, hate and anger and feel the love his father had for him.

But he realized that he'd missed those years of connecting with his father that he could have had.

This is the destructive power of holding onto grudges and the freedom it brings when you let them go.

Anytime you hold onto anything that keeps you feeling hurt, angry, upset or disconnected from someone else, the question we suggest you ask yourself is…

Is it worth it?

Is it worth it to hold onto an upset because someone didn't like the dress you wore to a party or the way you cut your hair?

Is it worth it to hold onto a grudge because you didn't get the raise in salary at work that you thought you deserved?

Is it worth it to hold onto a grudge because someone didn't follow through on a planned activity years ago and you believe they can't be trusted?

Is it worth it to hold onto anger that one or both of your parents didn't give you love in the way you thought they should have?

You may not realize it but by holding onto a grudge, you're actually creating a wall of anger and resentment (even though you may try to hold it in) that keeps you from feeling the truth of what was so upsetting, painful or hurtful.

The even weirder part of all of this is that by holding on to a grudge, you are also keeping the ill feelings alive inside you instead of choosing to let them go and enjoying the freedom you want from this person or situation that was painful to you.

And it stands in the way of understanding and forgiveness.

Holding onto a grudge is the exact opposite of what you want because you keep reliving whatever happened to upset you!

You might be thinking as you're reading this,

"All of this is helpful to know but hey, I don't hold onto grudges."

Well, guess what?

We're willing to bet that you do.

They may just be showing up in different forms or with different names.

You might be holding onto something your partner said two days ago and now you're not feeling like being very intimate when they suggest going to the bedroom for some fun.

You might respond with some sarcasm to something a co-worker or your boss at work said to you in last week's meeting and your sarcasm left them wondering, "Where'd that come from?"

Or

You might start coming home late or refuse to talk to your partner with as much kindness as you normally would because you didn't get your way with something you wanted.

Whether you call it a grudge or you call it something else, holding onto anything that keeps your heart closed almost never helps you get what you want in relationships.

Holding onto a grudge might seem like such a good strategy for avoiding emotional pain in the moment and possible pain in the future.

But this is the exact opposite of what is necessary to be open to more peace and love in all your relationships.

So, is there really a time when it's a good idea to hold onto anger and a grudge?

Yes, but only when you want to create more distance, separation and disconnection between you and someone else, punishing yourself in the process.

If you want more possibilities for love in your life, there is simply no room for grudges.

Grudges have got to go.

"When you're honest within yourself first, you can then make the choice to be honest with others or just let the thoughts and emotions go."

Susie Collins

Chapter 23
The First Person to be Honest With By Susie

I always thought I was an honest person and it was a shock to learn that I hadn't been with others and especially with myself.

During my first marriage that ended in divorce, I inwardly and with superiority frequently accused my then-husband of not being emotionally honest.

I thought I had it all together when it came to my feelings and that he didn't.

Throughout our entire marriage, I wanted him to "get in touch" with his feelings and thought that if he would be more emotionally aware, our marriage would be "saved" because I'd feel closer to him.

Years later, when I was with Otto, I was appalled to finally realize that in my experience, while my ex had trouble accessing his emotions, he wasn't the only one.

I found out that I wasn't always emotionally honest and hid what I was feeling on a regular basis.

"I'm fine" or "Nothing's wrong" came out of my mouth more often than not when I was really not allowing myself to feel whatever emotion that was lurking deep inside.

While my ex never challenged me about it, Otto did so in a loving way and helped me to see what I'd been habitually doing.

He challenged me to stop and feel what was inside instead of putting on my Super Woman cape and rushing into "fix it" mode.

Acknowledging what I was feeling didn't always mean I had to "do" something about it. Sometimes I needed to talk about something that was said or done and sometimes I could just feel it, seeing that what I was thinking might not be true and letting it go.

I realized that I'd been shutting off connection, not just with Otto but with others as well, because of my habit of skipping over my buried emotions that kept me from being more authentic.

Looking back, I realized that the tactic of trying to stay emotionally safe had driven a wedge between me and other people.

On some level, I was trying to be "perfect" and not show the real me I thought was flawed.

When thinking about honesty in a relationship, most people look outward at what the other person is doing while looking inward may be even more powerful.

When you're honest within yourself first, you can then make the choice to be honest with others or just let the thoughts and emotions go.

When you choose to look first at yourself with emotional honesty, there is a possibility for connection, not only with others, but with yourself.

When I started seeing that others, including Otto, wanted to connect with my authentic self and not the one I'd made up, my relationships and the love that surrounds me has deepened and expanded and it can do the same for you.

Self-honesty is a beautiful place to start creating more possibilities for love.

"If trying harder
doesn't work...
Try softer."

Lily Tomlin

Chapter 24
Relax Harder By Otto

I trained in the martial art Aikido for about 4 years and totally loved it.

I remember being at a two-day Aikido seminar and one of the black belts I was paired with to practice a certain move kept trying to get me to see how to do it in just the right way to produce a certain result.

Then, when I just wasn't getting it, the higher ranked student stopped his interactions and simply said this to me —

"Relax harder. You're not going to get this by forcing it. You're going to have to relax into it."

When my friend and Aikido partner said that to me, it was a game-changing moment for my martial arts training. I've also found it to be really instructive advice in the game of life and specifically relationships.

Relaxing, slowing down, and settling into a space where new possibilities can occur to you is game-changing and life-changing.

You can't shift a relationship or see possibilities when your mind is all revved up and you are trying to rush through or force something to happen.

It just won't work.

If you want to have deeper, more meaningful conversations, slow down and let them happen from natural curiosity.

If you want to have the person you can truly connect with come into your life, slow down.

"Don't dim your light just to keep the peace, fit in or hope for the best. In the long run, it never works! Always allow the light of who you are to shine for honest, heartfelt connections."

Otto Collins

Chapter 25
Loving Beyond People Pleasing

There's nothing wrong with wanting to please someone else.

But sometimes you just gotta stop it.

For more connection and love, you've got to stop and take a deeper look into why you want to please this person.

What's the real reason?

If you're like a lot of us, you could be trying to "please" someone in ways you THINK the other person wants in exchange for something you want in return.

In other words, it's really a back-handed way to get your needs met.

What you want could be love, attention, recognition, money, safety—anything.

The truth is that most "people pleasers" (and we've been there, too) are almost never aware that they're bending over backwards or going to extremes to try to make someone else happy. They simply aren't aware of the reasons they're doing it.

The truth is that you can enjoy authentic connections with others when you let go of people pleasing.

When you're so concerned with being on the lookout for what you think others want to hear, you completely miss connecting with them in a real way.

When you see how simply going along with what others want without looking at what you want builds resentment and shuts down the opportunity for others to know you better, you can recognize how this can be a form of hiding your true self to protect yourself from rejection or some other reason you've made up.

While none of this is conscious at the time, it just seems easier to agree.

But all it really does is build walls and keep you separate from the love of others.

It can be scary to let others see the real you and live your own life, so you keep trying to be who you think someone else wants you to be.

When you're in this game, you don't see that maybe you have it wrong and the other person would rather you be who you really are.

When you love beyond people pleasing, you can let go of the stress and the pressure of trying to get it "right" and live your life instead of trying to live through and for others.

The singer/songwriter Alicia Keys wrote a great song about being who she thought her boyfriend wanted her to be called "Gramercy Park."

Here are a few lines of this song:

"I've been doing all the things that I think you wanna see

I've been trying to fulfill you with your every need

Now you falling for a person that's not even me"

When you see that trying to get it right the way you think someone else wants you to be never works out in the end, you can let go of that pressure, relax and be who you truly are.

"How much love you've had in your relationships (and life) in the past has NOTHING to do with what's possible for you now."

Otto Collins

Chapter 26
Something Else By Otto

When people find out I'm a relationship and life coach and that I help people create more of what they want—not just in love, but all aspects of their lives—and they find out that I was married to someone else before Susie (for 15 years), a common question I get is this:

"Knowing what you now know about how to have a great relationship, do you think you could have saved your first marriage?"

People are shocked when I tell them the truth.

I say, "I don't think so."

And this is because in the final stages of agonizing about the question of whether to stay or go in that relationship, "Go" became the obvious and final answer every single time.

Not This

When most people think of possibilities, especially around love, they often have a really hard time saying or seeing what they want.

If they're not happy in their current situation, all they know is it's "not this."

It's "something else" that they can't even begin to know or understand.

Not yet anyway.

All they know is that this cry from inside for "something else" comes from the silent scream of an aching heart for more, much more.

Knowing that you want "something else" and NOT THIS is such a great starting place even if you don't know what the "something else" is.

If you let it settle and make it okay to emerge from your inner wanting, it will come.

In a relationship, "something else" doesn't have to mean it's time to find someone else as a partner.

It doesn't even have to mean something's wrong.

It could be that it's just an acknowledgement that something wants to come forth that isn't here yet.

It's a feeling of truth, an acknowledgement, a desire for the good, the beautiful and in some ways, the sacred you know at some level exists but isn't yet your reality.

It may be found right where you are after you let your guard down.

The "something else" you seek may be discovered in the shower or in the middle of eating tomorrow's breakfast.

Who knows?

I personally know several people whose relationships (and marriages) were essentially on life support who found a way to go from barely surviving to completely thriving.

A couple I'm thinking about in particular didn't know exactly what they wanted or what would "fix" things, but they knew they had problems and knew that they wanted more than they were currently experiencing.

They were open to what could be possible and were able to find the magic once again.

So can you in whatever form that might take.

Just know that anytime you start getting a nudge that there's "something else," it's the seed of something new wanting to emerge.

When you find yourself wanting something new, something different or something more alive, just remember this:

There are new possibilities in the words "Something else."

Chapter 27
Freeing Yourself from the "Shoulds"

How many times have you thought or said something like this to yourself or to someone else:

I "should" do this.

You "should" do that.

I "shouldn't" have to do this.

You "shouldn't" have to do that.

If you're living with a case of the "shoulds" (and almost everyone is), then welcome to being human.

So what's the problem?

When you're "shoulding" yourself, one of the things that's happening is you're trying to follow what you think someone else thinks is best for you in life or a situation and you're bypassing your own wisdom or desires. It's from a thought or belief about how life should be.

When you're "shoulding" someone else, you're imposing what you think is best for the other person (often without being asked) without really knowing if this course of action is best and if it's even your business in the first place.

The truth is that every "should" has its roots in a story or stories that might have some element of truth or may not.

It's all perception and we make it all up.

In relationships, this can play out in all kinds of ways and most of them aren't good if you want to create Big Fat Love.

We've had hundreds of coaching clients over the years say some version of this:

- "If he loved me, he should know what I want."
- "If she loved me, she shouldn't talk to other men at parties."
- "Because my adult kid is about to make a big mistake, he should do what I say."

Or

- "I shouldn't have to open my heart to her after all she's done to me," totally missing the importance of keeping your heart open as a path to healing the past.

Some of our friends and family members have shut off the possibilities to more love in their lives because of one event that happened or one thing someone said to them in the past that created a strong limiting belief that turned into a "should" or a "shouldn't."

One friend almost missed out on the best, most amazing relationship of his life because of his belief that any partner he would want to be with "should" be within six years of his age.

For the longest time, his thinking was really solid which prohibited him from considering someone if she was outside of this age range.

We're really glad he chose to disregard this "should" because the woman he ended up being with for several years turned out to be eight years younger than him and they had an incredible relationship until he passed in a tragic accident.

Anytime you're using the word "should," you are making a judgment about how something should or shouldn't be in order for you to be OK.

Whether it's with you or someone else, when you're coming from a place of the "shoulds," you've made up a meaning about how something should or shouldn't be and that almost never comes from a place of possibility.

It almost always comes from your past thinking, your past beliefs, your past pain and your past ways of coping, of making yourself feel safe. "Shoulds" often stem from your habits of being that you learned from someone else or from past situations that have absolutely nothing to do with right now.

We once heard Dr Joe Vitale ask a really thought-provoking question that points to the heart of the problem of living from the "shoulds."

His question was this:

"Are you living from memory or inspiration?"

Any time you are living from or acting from a "should," you're living from memory and not from a clean slate to create something special.

Living from inspiration is looking at this moment with openness and totally new eyes.

The truth is that BIG FAT LOVE (in any kind of relationship) is never created from the "shoulds."

It's created right here, right now in a brand new moment that's full of possibilities.

We invite you to challenge your "shoulds" in whatever form they take and start from a place of openness to something new, some other possibility and something special in each moment.

Then, as you do that, you'll start noticing in big and small ways, all the miracles that can come from living from inspiration and love instead of judgment, pre-suppositions, doubts and the "shoulds."

"It takes the same amount of energy to have a great marriage as it does an average one."

Grant Cardone

Chapter 28
Winning the "What If" Game

There's a game we all play with ourselves all the time, mostly without realizing it.

This game is what we call, the "What If" game.

There are two ways to play the "What If" game and the quantity and quality of love you can give and receive depends on how you choose to play.

One way is "What If Down" and the second is "What If Up."

We ask ourselves "What If Down" questions all the time like these:

- "What if he won't love me anymore if I don't do what he wants?"
- "What if I'm not being a good daughter if I don't bring my mother to my house for dinner every night?"

Or

- "What if I say 'no' to my friend's invitation because I really want to stay home but she won't like me anymore if I do?"

"What If Down" shows up in our thinking in so many other ways too.

For example:

- "What if he finds someone more attractive than me?"
- "What if we get bored with each other?"
- "What if we run out of things to talk about?"
- "What if he really doesn't love me like he says he does?"
- "What if this argument we're having just gets worse and worse?"
- "What if she stops wanting to have sex with me?"
- "What if there really is a reason not to trust her?"
- "What if he stops finding me attractive?"
- "What if our communication never gets better?"
- "What if her spending habits keep us from being able to do the things I want to do?"

We could go on and on but you get the idea.

These almost automatic inner questions limit love with the focus being on fear and what's not wanted rather than what is wanted.

Sounds like a no-brainer to avoid these types of questions, doesn't it?

So what would be better?

Refocusing your negative thoughts on "What If Up" questions would be WAY better.

So, what would be some "What If Up" questions that can encourage possibilities of authenticity, connection, ease and deeper love?

Here are a few we came up with to get your creativity going:

- "What if there's another way to provide my mother with dinner each evening?"
- "What if I can be honest and say 'no' with love?"
- "What if there's a way that would work for both of us?"
- "What if communication could be easier?"
- "What if there's something we can do to make our love even stronger?"
- "What if I opened my heart a little more instead of closing it when I get triggered?"
- "What if there isn't anything to fear here even though my head is spinning all these negative stories?"
- "What if being with our kids could make us appreciate our love even more?"
- "What if he's really NOT giving me any reason to think the worst?"
- "What if I can open to understanding and finding out more instead of jumping to conclusions?"

It's a simple idea really.

If you're going to play the "What If" game, then why not play it in a way that builds more love, intimacy and connection instead of focusing on what can destroy love in your life?

Our invitation to you is to consciously choose whether you want to let the "what if down" game run your life or choose the vast possibilities of "What If Up."

The prospect of more love, peace and happiness in your life depends on it.

"Nothing ever goes
away until it teaches us
what we need to know."

Pema Chodron

Chapter 29
Stop Believing Your Own BS

Let's say you're having a thought that everything about love is hard.

And let's say that every relationship you've ever been in has been difficult and you're just sick and tired of it being such hard work.

Maybe you think it's always going to be this way.

Because of all this thinking, you throw your hands up in the air and think to yourself, "If love is going to be this way, then I'm not going to play."

Then you become defensive, resentful, shut down and stop opening to new possibilities whether you're with someone or not.

Your pattern at that point might be to defend, protect your heart and make sure you don't do anything that might cause you to get "hurt" again.

We've discovered it's all BS.

It's all stories.

It's all a creation of the mind.

It's all created by your mind as a way of protecting yourself from something bad happening.

If you want more possibilities in love and life, one of the most important things you can start doing right now is to stop believing your own bullshit (or BS).

By BS, we mean anything you're thinking and believing that may or may not be true that is getting in the way of more love.

Unless there's actual physical or emotional abuse going on for you, there's never anything you need to protect yourself from except for what you make up as a problem in your life.

As an example:

As of the time we're writing this, this is our 25th year together. We've both been through previous marriages that ended in divorce and both of us agree that this has been 25 years filled with deep connection and love that has surpassed anything we could have ever thought possible.

We both chose to see the breakups of our previous marriages (as painful as the breakups were) as blessings and doorways to something greater.

But many people who go through a breakup take their relationship ending and all the emotion surrounding it as a sign to not open to love any more.

In fact, we know someone who was so traumatized by a breakup she didn't want more than twenty years ago, she's never been on a "date" with someone else in all that time.

Which is true?

Is a breakup a blessing and a doorway to something new, something better and possibly something amazing or is it a sign telling you not to open your heart to love anymore?

The answer is this:

Neither one.

You get to decide what is true in your life and your world.

Any time you tell yourself anything that gets in the way of a new possibility of love, it isn't a fact.

It can't be.

It's just a story that you've made up to support your thinking you've turned into your reality.

If you want more love in your life and you want to open to new possibilities around love, then stop it.

Stop believing anything that would have you believe anything else but the best possibility for you.

Want new love in your life?

Then choose to believe only thoughts you have that support that.

Want better communication, more trust and deeper intimacy?

Then only believe your thoughts that support more of what you want instead of all the BS your mind makes up to support a lack of love or possibilities.

None of us knows the future, but as we've said many times in this book,

You can be open to seeing what's possible that you actually might want instead of what you don't want.

When you stop worrying about what you have no control over, what your fears or doubts are telling you and simply stop ruminating over anything that takes you away from new possibilities for love, you open yourself to noticing those possibilities that are already there in every moment.

The great thing about being in this human body and having this human experience is how awesome it is to get to choose what's important to you and what's not.

You get to decide what you're going to believe and make real and what story you're going to call bullshit on.

You get to choose.

We think that's good to know and it's also an awesome way to go through life—knowing that we are the ones with the power to choose what's BS and what isn't.

When you see this for yourself, all kinds of new love possibilities start to open up for you.

"You don't have
to control your
thoughts. You just
have to stop letting
them control you."

Dan Millman

Chapter 30
Commitment as a Joyous Choice

Otto's mother has had so many friends and family members die from cancer over the years that she won't even say the word "cancer."

She calls it the "c" word.

There's another "c" word that far too many people don't want to talk about and it's "commitment.

People don't want to talk about it because of the meaning they've made up about it and what it means about them, their partner, the people in their life and love as a whole.

We've had hundreds of conversations with coaching clients over the years about commitment who've said something to us like THIS:

"I'm committed to the relationship, but I'm just miserable and I'm only staying because I made a commitment."

Or

"I'm committed to the relationship, but I'm not sure my partner is."

Or a really big one

"I'm committed because even if I'm not happy, I have so many years invested in this relationship and I don't want to start over."

This just seems like a horrible way to live and love.

Not because we think you shouldn't be committed to a particular person or committed to staying in a particular relationship.

That's not it at all.

It's because of a distinction we heard once from Kellen Fluckinger who said,

"Commitment can be a joyous choice instead of a painful chain."

If you're committed and you're in a challenging relationship, staying in love and staying in the relationship can be painful, especially if you're locked in a struggle that appears to have no end.

But, what if you changed your whole outlook and definition of commitment?

- What if "commitment" or "being committed" didn't have to be a struggle?

- What if commitment didn't have to be exhausting or test your will to stay in the relationship?

- What if you saw commitment as a joyous choice in the moment instead of a painful chain or something that's meant to bind or imprison you?

- What if a commitment was something you could change or renegotiate if it no longer worked for you?

- What if the only commitment is saying "yes" to the present moment?

We get it.

We know there are many people who fervently believe that commitment isn't supposed to be easy.

These people believe that if committing to someone or something was easy, then it wouldn't be commitment.

These people believe that if the relationship commitment wasn't "forced on you," then when times get tough, it would be so easy just to bail out on the relationship.

And we don't have any argument about all this except for one very big thing.

It's the fact that you have at least two choices about how to see commitment.

You can see it as something akin to prison or you can see commitment as a choice that you make in every moment.

Wow.

There's a big difference between being committed because you made a decision and you're bound by that decision versus being committed because it's a choice you're making in this moment.

When you see commitment as a joyous choice you make to someone or something you think is worth making a commitment to, everything changes.

There's more peace.

New possibilities begin to emerge and options for resolving any challenges become easier simply because you are remaining open to something new potentially emerging.

"When you choose to love someone as they are and not how you think they should be, there's greater trust and deeper communication than you ever thought possible."

Susie Collins

Chapter 31
It's Not Your Job By Susie

Many years ago, after my father's major heart attack, I thought we were going to lose him.

He was frail, struggling to breathe, and couldn't walk very far on his own.

From what I was seeing, if he didn't change his ways of eating and living, he wouldn't be with us very much longer.

I thought I had to do something to help him change and started pressuring him to eat healthier foods.

From personal experience and from a lot of self-study about nutrition and health, I thought I could "save" him if he would only change his eating habits.

One day after several months of my badgering, he looked in my eyes and quietly told me that he didn't want to eat that way in the time he had left.

I listened and felt his love because that was one of the few emotionally honest moments I'd had with him my entire life.

I stopped my nagging and let go of my desire to change him.

The truth is that no one ever really wants to change unless it's their idea, including you.

In spite of this, when we, as humans, think we have a better idea for someone else, we want them to change to our way of thinking.

While it's what most of us do, you've probably seen how hard it can be, if not impossible, to "change" someone's way of thinking and acting.

If you've guilt tripped, manipulated or used any other method of trying to get another person to change, you've most likely run into resistance, stubbornness, defensiveness and a brick wall.

Resistance is the enemy of change and people resist any time it doesn't make sense to them or it isn't their idea.

They may feel controlled and become entrenched even more deeply in "being right" according to their thinking.

To have lasting change, a person has to see something new for himself or herself.

Changing, shifting or taking on a new behavior or a new way of doing things never happens until and unless it seems like a good idea to the person.

Here's what I've found:

No matter how much you want to, it's not your job to change another human being.

It's not your job to fix them and, despite what you might think, they don't need fixing.

It's not your job to change them so you can be okay which, if you're honest, may ultimately be the reason you want that person to change.

I realized that when I urged my father to eat healthier foods without him asking for my help, what I really wanted was for him to live longer than the few months he'd been told by the doctors.

I knew our family would completely change with his loss and as futile as it was, I didn't want that to happen so soon.

I worried that our family wouldn't be okay, especially me, when he passed.

But when he spoke his truth to me, I saw that I could honor how he wanted to live the rest of his life and let go of what I thought he should do.

If you want your partner or anyone to change, show up as love and ask if he or she wants your help. Make a request and be an invitation to something bigger or better that they may not be able to see for themselves.

And it has to be their choice to see it or not.

Does that mean you have to shut up and put up with "bad" behavior?

Of course not! You have a choice as well.

You can decide how important your desired changes for the other person are to you and embrace the possibility that maybe you can be open to changing as well.

- It might be that you see something new in that you don't have to hold on so tightly to how you think things "should" be.
- It might be that you see that it doesn't have to be exactly the way you want it to be for you to be happy.
- It might also be that the change you want to see in your partner or in someone else is a deal breaker for you if it doesn't happen.

True change is an inside job, whether it's you or the other person you want to change.

When YOU start shifting and changing, your relationship will change and the other person will have the opportunity to change as well.

When you choose to love someone as they are and not how you think they should be, there's greater trust and deeper communication than you ever thought possible.

Chapter 32
Your Partner is Not the Enemy By Otto

I couldn't help overhearing the conversation at the table next to mine when the man very sharply said to his wife, "Stop it. Just stop it," as she asked him questions about the food items on the menu.

The restaurant is a regional favorite, famous for its unique flavor in the food items they offer.

This woman's husband used to live in the area and was familiar with the food options, but because she was from another part of the country, she was not.

In this moment, all it appeared this woman was doing was getting curious and a little bit excited about what might be on the menu of this restaurant her husband had been talking about for many years.

With his words and tone of voice, it was obvious that he squelched her questions and excitement right then and there.

This was both fascinating and tragic to me because just moments earlier when they came in to be seated, I saw the two of them struggling with the simple question from the server of "table or booth."

He said "table" and she said "booth" and as the server turned to lead them to the nearest available booth, the man mumbled, "I guess I just never get my way," loud enough that anyone within earshot could hear them.

With the server's help, the couple finally placed their order. The server scooped up their menus and the woman tightly smiled and excused herself to go to the rest room.

While she was gone, I couldn't help but strike up a quick conversation with the woman's husband.

I learned they were from Greenville, South Carolina, some 450 miles away from Columbus, Ohio where we were sitting.

They were on their way to Cleveland, Ohio to the Rock and Roll Hall of Fame as part of their weekend trip to celebrate their sixth wedding anniversary.

I saw there was love there. But, there was also anger, the dance of superiority/inferiority, as well as obvious signs of contempt.

Because of the contempt and other struggles I could see this couple was going through, my "Spidey" senses told me that even though they loved and cared for each other, danger lies ahead for them.

If something doesn't change between the two of them, if they don't see something new about how to love each other, and if they don't stop making each other wrong and the "enemy," there probably won't be a seventh anniversary trip next year.

In all the different parts of our lives, so many of us go "unconscious" and without realizing what we're doing, we make the other people in our lives the enemy then we wonder where the love and connection went that used to feel so good.

It's easy to do.

You find some aspect of the other person you think ought to be changed or improved and out of your desire to make them better, of course, you let them know about their faults and shortcomings.

You keep finding things they need to "work on" or improve and before long, anger, resentment and feelings of being unloved or unappreciated creep in.

Or maybe you're just irritated with work, hungry or feel physically or emotionally unwell and you take it out on the person closest to you.

Then, usually without thinking, the other person responds with one or more of the "Three F's" (fight, flight or freeze) to your unwelcome, critical judgments.

One evening during the period of time when Susie and I were writing this book, we were getting ready to drive to an arts festival in another part of the city, when she asked me,

"Is it going to get chilly tonight?"

My instant response was,

"I don't know. I'll check the weather for you."

When I got my phone out to check the weather, I told Susie it was going to be about 70 degrees at 11 pm and she could use that as her guide.

When I said that, I got really emotional. And the emotions came for two reasons:

One: The conversation and scene I witnessed with the man and the woman at the restaurant was still fresh in my mind.

I realized that when Susie asked me about the weather, unlike the man at the restaurant, I answered with kindness and love.

Two: I was also emotional because I realized there have been times in other relationships, as well as times with Susie, when I've responded in unkind and unloving ways.

But this night I didn't.

As you read this, please don't read this as "about me" and think I'm looking for a "pat on the back" or for you to think I did something great.

That's not the point.

The point is that on this occasion, it would have been so easy to make my partner the enemy and say something unkind like, "How should I know? Look it up yourself."

But I didn't do that. That's exactly the kind of remark that would starve love, not nourish it.

The real point is that you, me and everyone else has a fresh new opportunity in every moment to love the people in our lives and NOT make them the enemy like we might be tempted to do.

Is love really supposed to be a "battlefield," as the song by Pat Benatar goes?

Only if we make our loved one the enemy.

We also have the opportunity in every moment to show up as kindness and love, to build love, to build connection and keep our hearts open which, in turn, will keep their hearts open as well.

Love is always here and always available.

Love is a constant, continuous creation that can happen even if you may not feel physically or emotionally healthy or "up to par."

As one of our teachers says, "No one is worthy of your judgment and everyone is worthy of your love."

No relationship is ever brought closer when one (or both people) turn the other into the enemy instead of someone to be loved and appreciated.

It just takes deciding how you want to "be" in the moment and if love is your answer, to act from that place with those closest to you.

Chapter 33
Laughing Out Loud

A couple of summers ago we had a big problem with squirrels burying their nuts in the flower pots on our front porch.

They would dig them out to have something to eat, destroying the flowers planted in those pots in the process.

In an earlier time in his life, Otto might have trapped them, poisoned them or tried to hit them with something to help them get the idea we wanted them to stay out of our flower pots and stop destroying our flowers.

These days, he's much kinder to all sentient beings and none of those things were an option.

We needed a solution.

So, what did Otto do?

He tore the lid off of a cardboard box and took a black Sharpie marker and in big bold letters wrote the words:

"Squirrels, Keep Out!"

Then, he took the cardboard and stapled it to a small stake and put it in the biggest flower pot.

At the time, Susie doubled over in laughter at the idea that the squirrels, first of all could read the sign and second of all, do as we were asking on the sign and "keep out" of our flowers.

It may be hard to believe, but whether it was the sign that did it or the power of our intention, from that point on and for the rest of the summer, the squirrels stayed out of those flower pots and what flowers remained, survived gloriously.

On the surface, this might have seemed like a really dumb idea. But even if it didn't work, the one thing it did do is keep us laughing the rest of that summer every time we saw that sign.

We've seen that laughing together is something that brings us closer and it's not just true for us.

We're willing to bet it's true for you in your relationships too.

If you want to increase love and possibilities in your life, one of the suggestions we always make is to laugh louder and more often.

Even if you're not one of those "laugh-out-loud" types, you can find your own way of laughing and having a good time that brings you closer to those you love.

Notice we didn't say laughing AT someone. We're talking about laughing with someone.

What we're pointing to is how you can always find things to laugh about if you look for them.

Otto has a habit of taking screenshots on his phone of what he finds humorous and sharing them with Susie and she usually finds them funny as well.

We'll also send a funny emoji to each other during the day that brings a smile or a laugh.

One couple we know made an agreement that whenever they started noticing they were having an argument, they would immediately take off all their clothes. They found they fell into giggles and it was much more difficult to be mad at the other while naked rather than fully clothed.

We're not suggesting you do this (unless you want to) but instead, we're suggesting that you consciously and deliberately look for the funny, the humorous and in some cases, the irreverently ridiculous to laugh about.

One thing we know for sure is you can't be fighting or arguing about something while you're laughing.

Of course, there are issues that you want and need to talk about but solutions don't come to the surface when you're stuck in an argument.

Possibilities happen much more easily when you break up the tension with laughter.

Finding things to be critical of, upset about or wrong about the other person shrivels up possibilities and this includes sarcasm which most people don't enjoy or find funny, especially when it's directed their way.

The idea of finding more things to laugh about may seem like such simple advice that you may be wondering why we're even talking about this.

We're talking about it because what we've seen is that one of the first things to go when problems start cropping up in a relationship is the fun and the laughter.

Finding things to laugh about on a regular basis creates more connection and makes being together more fun.

It also expands your possibilities for more love, better relationships and a happier life.

"I want to be in a relationship where you telling me you love me is just a ceremonious validation of what you already show me."

Steve Maraboli

Chapter 34
Sex, Pleasure and Passion

No matter what your experience has been up until now, when it comes to passion, intimacy and yes, even great sex, the possibilities are much greater than you have imagined.

What if the amount of passion you and your partner brought to the relationship was not something that just happened but was a deliberate choice made by the two of you?

What if you just decided that lovemaking and sex were priorities?

How would that decision change things?

If you were to believe everything you find on the internet, you'd be led to believe by some "experts" that it's possible to keep the passion red hot forever.

And to that we say,

Maybe.

But for most people it goes like this:

You get together with someone and in the beginning the passion and attraction that borders on lust is off the charts.

In this "honeymoon" phase, you typically can't get enough of each other and then, even though you still love each and want to be together, "Life" happens.

Over time, the attraction and passion begin to fizzle, fading out to the point that one or both of you start looking for the "on switch" again.

Yes, there is such a thing as "chemistry."

We had it in the beginning of our relationship and we still have it.

Millions of other couples around the world have it too.

Chemistry is when two people just "click" or gel.

There's not one way to describe it other than when you're with someone and you have chemistry, being together just feels right, it feels good and often you feel connected in multiple ways, both in and out of the bedroom.

The problem with chemistry is that you can't rely on it alone to sustain and grow your relationship through the years.

As we've said, you have to keep feeding the relationship and any chemistry you have together.

Far too many people think that when the intensity and passion start to fade a little bit (or maybe a lot), this means way more about passion and their relationship than it needs to.

When the chemistry seems off, people often think the relationship is in trouble, needs help or worse.

We've found that the most important thing to know about chemistry is that you can recreate it.

Just like high school chemistry, you can change the "chemical compounds" you're using and turn them up just as easily as you can allow passion to fade away or dissipate.

You can decide to connect deeper, open more, be more vulnerable, more playful and choose to increase desire.

There's also something to be said for the importance of deciding how much passion you want and how much you are willing to open to it and prioritize the time for it.

Of course, there can be an ebb and flow to your sex life as your body and your priorities change, but that doesn't have to limit your enjoyment.

When you see that passion is a choice, EVERYTHING can change.

Then, when you see that everything about passion, intimacy and sex is a creation:

- You get to decide what's appropriate and what isn't.
- You get to decide how much and how often.
- You get to decide what a boundary is and what isn't.
- You get to decide what would be fun to explore in the bedroom and what wouldn't.
- You get to decide what's sexy and what isn't.
- You get to decide whether something is too vulgar, too risky or scary to consider trying in the bedroom or whether trying it would be a total turn on.
- You get to decide whether you're too old or too anything to have passion still be a vital part of your life.

No one else gets to decide that for you.

The plain truth is that you get to decide how much passion you want in your life.

And if you're with a partner, they get a voice in that as well.

If you are not in an intimate relationship or marriage or your partner is unwilling, you can still choose to make sex, pleasure and passion an important part of your life.

There is no rule that says only people in relationships with willing partners get to enjoy pleasure, fun, excitement and sex.

Sex for one can also be exciting. There are entire books written on the subject that are worth exploring.

Consensual sex, intimacy, fun and pleasure either in (or not in) a committed relationship can be amazing and such an awesome part of your life, but many people choose to shut it off or allow it to fade away when they don't have to.

For us, the question is this:

Will it be more fun, more exciting and more enjoyable to keep the passion, excitement and love hot and growing than to let it die or fade away?

To us and hopefully for you too, this is a no-brainer.

It's aliveness and passion for sure.

"What if you never stopped flirting?"

Otto Collins

Chapter 35
Never Stop Flirting

It's a fact.

People flirt with each when they're attracted to one another.

They flirt when they're new in their relationship.

They flirt when they're newly married or "committed."

People flirt when they want to rekindle the spark.

But what if you never stopped flirting?

What if you always looked for the fun, the playful, the sexy, the excitement and erotic in the other?

What would be possible if you never stopped flirting?

We're guessing there wouldn't be any limit to the increase in passion, fun and yes, even exciting sex when you consciously decided to allow yourself to genuinely flirt each day.

Continuing to flirt with your partner feeds the relationship and shows that it's important to you!

Flirting can be anything that fuels interest and excitement from a loving text to a surprise kiss at unexpected times.

Here's what Linda, one of our early readers of this book, said —

"For over eleven years I've been with my amazing and loving partner, and you're right—you gotta feed that love between meals. In the car we still do a 'red light challenge' and lean in for a kiss before the light changes. We send emoji texts during his workday (I'm retired, he's not). I couldn't even list all the small things, a wink or a smile or a funny 'hubba-hubba' eyebrow dance when I head to the shower. Love doesn't feel like something to conform to anymore, but something that, as you point out, responds to nourishment and attention. I see the connection now of giving and receiving loving attention, not just to remind him that I love him but to activate my love in the giving. I feel cherished when he stands on the porch step so he can stand on the lower one (he's taller than me) for a long kiss that makes the neighbors cringe, I bet! Just thinking about love as abundant, limitless, expanding, and BIG AND FAT makes me feel like, hey, I'm in! That's for me!"

Whether you're in a committed relationship (or you want to be in one), do not underestimate the fun and possibilities that flirting can bring to your love life.

The two of us flirt with each other constantly and that's one important ingredient in keeping our love big and fat!

So how can you include flirting with your significant other as an important part of your relationship?

Chapter 36
Celebrate More Often

Here's what might be a new possibility for expanding love:

Find more opportunities to celebrate love, life and the people you're in relationship with.

Open to expanding your definition of celebration to include more than the usual anniversaries and standard holidays.

Open to seeing that a celebration can be broader than giving a gift or going to a restaurant for dinner.

Celebrate the small things as Elin, one of our early readers of this book, told us…

"Celebrate the small things. It's easy to focus on the big fancy stuff but the magic is in the everyday mini miracles. The time I have with my boyfriend is limited so I celebrate every time we get to wake up together. I have shared this with him and remind him of how special it is for me to wake up with him every time we get the chance to do so."

As Elin said, the "magic is in the everyday mini miracles" and a celebration is an acknowledgement of those miracles as they happen.

A celebration can be words of appreciation after noticing that someone you love has followed through on a promise when you may have thought he or she wouldn't.

A celebration can be noticing when someone says or does something that's kind to you and supports you and then speaking words of acknowledgement.

A celebration can be acknowledging yourself for not getting defensive when you might have in the past.

A celebration can be acknowledging yourself when you see the good in your beloved instead of what's less desirable to you.

Celebrate how far you've come in your love for yourself and for each other.

Celebrate the fact that you have been gifted with the ability to love.

Celebrate the normal, the mundane, the beautiful, the small simple acts as well as the bigger ones.

Celebrate how you can show up as love in this moment.

Celebrate everything (even the painful parts) because they taught you important lessons.

And the reason you celebrate everything is that when you do, more openness, love and aliveness is created.

When you don't celebrate, you're not seeing the gifts of love and abundance that you've already been given.

When you don't celebrate, you miss the opportunity for connection.

When you don't celebrate and something amazing passes you by, you're allowing yourself to lapse into unconscious behaviors from the past that disconnect you from others.

When the two of us celebrate each other or someone else, it just feels good.

It creates a vibration of love.

And that's something we can all use.

Our encouragement to you is this:

Celebrate more.

Celebrate more love.

Celebrate each other.

Celebrate yourself.

Celebrate this moment.

Celebrate the past.

Celebrate your failures.

Celebrate your successes.

Celebrate the people in your life.

Celebrate everything.

Possibilities will grow and expand when you do.

"You can't go back and change the beginning, but you can start where you are and change the ending."

C.S. Lewis

Chapter 37
Gracious Endings in Love and Life

Here's a question we've spent a lot of time thinking about and maybe you've wondered about this too:

Why is it that some people go through life and really struggle with "endings" and others seem to go through those times with less stress and more ease?

What if you could have gracious endings instead of ugly, messy and painful ones?

What if intimate relationships, friendships, jobs or anything else could end as normal, natural and smooth as the sun coming up in the morning and the sun going down in the evening?

The truth is that endings come in all shapes and sizes and in different times in our lives.

And they are just a part of life.

How we go through them and our acceptance of the reality of them makes all the difference in our ability for happiness and love in the present moment and in our future.

Gracious endings can occur as a result of an intersection between what is wanted and what is no longer wanted.

They can happen because you see beyond the pain and loss to the reality of what is.

When you're faced with an ending that you might not have wanted and you're holding onto regret and being right, you're creating suffering that you don't have to keep alive.

You might be still fighting for what you wanted but didn't get.

You might be arguing that it shouldn't have been that way but it was.

You may be deep in anxiety, pain and regret and can't see any way out.

But the way out is to only recognize that it all will pass, if you allow it.

The two of us have had many gracious endings as well as a few ungracious ones in our lives and Susie's divorce from her first husband was one of the gracious ones.

She and her previous husband both looked back on their 30 years together with appreciation while also looking toward the future where they each wanted something different from what they had together.

Maybe one of the best examples of a gracious ending from our lives happened about a year after we got together.

The two of us were attending what might be called a New Age expo in another city and we ran into a woman whom Otto had dated briefly after he left his first wife.

As this woman and Otto briefly talked, she told him that it was clear what her role was in his life—to show him what was possible in a relationship and to be a bridge to the relationship he truly wanted.

They parted with total love and appreciation for each other and their time together.

That was a gracious ending and a completion.

But what if there's no completion, the ending is abrupt and you were blindsided and didn't want it?

Sure, there can be grief and allowing yourself to grieve a loss is healthy.

And you can also make a choice to look toward the possibilities of your future, even one moment at a time, and not carry regret or hang onto what was or what could have been.

You can allow yourself to come to a completion and peace inside you, recognizing that the grief will pass if you allow it.

You can acknowledge what you learned from that relationship and experience and let it go with love.

Early in our relationship, one of the first trips we took together was a trip to Maine. While planning the trip and then while on the trip itself, we felt the need to create some form of ritual of completion of our first marriages so we could consciously move on with ours.

So there we were, standing on Bald Head Cliff in Maine, with fierce and intense, pounding waves of the Atlantic Ocean crashing around us. Feeling the beauty and sacredness of the moment, we blessed and appreciated our previous relationships. Then we tossed our wedding rings from those marriages into the rolling sea underneath us.

This was a way to symbolically and energetically create a gracious ending and a powerful beginning.

Gracious endings aren't just possible for us, but for you as well if you open to the ending with love.

The "how" of a gracious ending isn't important at all.

It doesn't have to be any kind of ritual or big production. In fact, no one has to ever know about your particular process of letting go of the old to say a bigger "yes" to the new.

What is important in any ending is the spirit of your intention and the willingness of the letting go so you can look forward.

That's where the possibilities are created.

"Under the anger, under the fear, under the despair, under the broken-heartedness, there is a radiance that has never been harmed, that has never been lost, that is the truth of who you are."

Gangaji

Chapter 38

Love is Who We Are

If someone were to say to you "Love is who you are," you might be tempted to not believe them.

But what if this is actually true?

What if love is who you are—always available, always abundant and always flowing through and around you?

What if the only thing limiting the amount of love you can give or receive in this life is you?

What if your ability to love and be loved is limited only by the walls, defenses and barriers you put up within and around you to protect yourself from the possibility of love not working out?

So we end this book of love and possibilities the way we started it by saying this:

Love isn't something you have to "get."

Love is our nature.

It is our birthright.

It's always here.

It's who we are.

You just have to see that.

About the Authors

We're Susie and Otto Collins, spiritual and life partners, and since 1999 we've been sharing a simple message of hope and love with people all over the world.

The two of us are Certified Transformative Coaches who can help you move past stress, challenges, conflict and misunderstandings and into a life with love and possibilities.

Over the years we've created *Magic Relationship Words*, *No More Jealousy*, *Relationship Trust Turnaround* and many other books and programs, plus our Love Made Easy Podcast that helps people have stress-free relationships that are filled with love.

Although we've been featured on many national and international media outlets like, Men's Fitness magazine, Huffington Post, BBC and Yahoo shine--our real passion is connecting with people like you and doing whatever we can to help you create more love in your life and more life in your love.

If you're someone who wants less stress and more ease, flow and love in your relationships and life, learn more about how you can work with us to create some new possibilities.

Contact us for a conversation with one of us to help see those new possibilities at our website https://susieandotto.com/contact/

Listen to episodes of our Love Made Easy Podcast and check out our Blog for many free articles on a wide variety of relationship topics.

Please know that no matter what your relationships have been like up until now, you can have all the love you could ever want if you're open to seeing some new possibilities.

Acknowledgements

Our goal in writing this book is to make it the best resource possible for expanding love and possibilities in your life and we couldn't have done that alone.

Although we wrote every word, we couldn't have been able to share what's within these pages without our own willingness and commitment to learn from our teachers, guides and mentors through the years and then incorporate these truths and ideas into our own relationship, life and our one-on-one coaching work with others.

Some of these guides mentors and teachers we mention in the book but we want to specifically acknowledge Gangaji, "The Work" of Byron Katie, Abraham-Hicks , *The Way of Mastery* , Michael Singer, Michael Neill, Paul Selig (and the guides), and the teachings of Sydney Banks and Steve Hardison.

Also, we want to thank and acknowledge our early readers of BIG FAT LOVE who gave us so much incredible feedback that made this book a MUCH better read. These people include Heather Quick, Elin Crotty, Nancy Pringle, Mary Greenlee, Emma Cram, David Frey, Robert Scott, Linda Blaine, Li Shen, Lauren Redmond, Alison Forche and Mara Holt.

A big thank you to Amy Phillips-Gary for editing the final draft of this book, Linda Blaine for her back cover suggestions and edits and to Roberta Kayne for her back cover photograph.

Last of all, thank you for your openness, willingness and desire to expand your possibilities for love in your life.

The world needs more love and not less.

This expansion of love starts with each one of us in each moment.

Making Love Last: Creating Your Vision for Lasting Love

In this audio, we're talking about the big reasons why some relationships stay close, connected and loving forever and others don't.

We're answering the question, "Why is it that some people are able to keep their love going and create true lasting love that stands the test of time and other people don't?"

We're also exploring the question, "Why do some couples seem to be happy, still connected and still in love even after many years of being together and other couples seem to almost come to hate each other?"

You'll hear us discuss our radical answers to:

- How to have lasting love.
- What lasting love is and what it's not.
- How to love more in each moment.
- And much more.

Get this free audio at SusieAndOtto.com/bookbonus.

Printed in Great Britain
by Amazon

39335394R00099